£29.95

INNOVATION AND INDUSTRIAL STRENGTH

INNOVATION AND INDUSTRIAL STRENGTH

A study in the United Kingdom, West Germany, the United States and Japan

JOAN COX and HERBERT KRIEGBAUM

Policy Studies Institute
in association with
the Anglo-German Foundation

338. 06 C

PSI Publications are obtainable from all good bookshops, or by visiting the Institute at 100 Park Village East, London NW1 3SR (01-387 2171).

Sales Representation: Pinter Publishers Ltd.

Individual and Bookshop orders to: Marston Book Services Ltd, PO Box 87, Oxford, OX4 1LB.

A CIP catalogue record of this book is available from the British Library

PSI Research Report 691

ISBN 0 85374 458 0

Typeset by Policy Studies Institute

Printed in Great Britain by BPCC Wheaton Ltd., Exeter

Contents

Tables

Part III   Summary and conclusions

Appendix A

Appendix B

Appendix C

Figures

Preface and acknowledgements

The forerunner to this study was funded by the Anglo-German Foundation for the Study of Industrial Society, and the findings were published in 1980 under the title, *Growth, innovation and employment: an Anglo-German comparison.*

In 1985, the National Economic Development Office and the Confederation of British Industry suggested to the Foundation that it would be useful to update the study and extend the analysis to countries other than Britain and Germany. The Foundation agreed to support a new project to include comparable analyses for the United States and Japan and for a fifth industry, electronics. The present book is based on the broader study and the Foundation's support is gratefully acknowledged.

To undertake research into the inner workings of manufacturing industries in several countries, one requires friends and many of them. Research of this kind goes through many stages – finding the data, assembling them for computer analysis and finally the interpretation. We had the most generous help at every stage.

Our first thanks must go to our research assistant Kevin Goldberg who designed the analytical system and combed the libraries for up to 20 years of data. To members of the Directorate for Science, Technology and Industry at OECD in Paris we offer thanks for their help, both in assembling data and for their interpretation of international trends; also to Jacques Sassoon of the British Library, Japanese Information Service, for his translations of Japanese texts. Our grateful thanks also go to Graham Clements who, with the greatest patience and fortitude over many months, read and criticised successive drafts.

Finally our warmest thanks go to colleagues at PSI, especially Sir Charles Carter for his challenging comments on our various economic heresies and Peter Willmott for editorial advice and help.

Synopsis

The objective of the analysis described in this book is to discover why some industries succeed and others do not, and the part that technological change plays in success.

The book first discusses the concept of economic performance and how it should be measured. Performance is shown to be a parameter that is impossible to encapsulate in one indicator: it requires the simultaneous assessment of both long-term and short-term cash movements which must remain in a delicate balance with cash receipts. Put another way, manufacturing firms remain in business because they receive funds from their customers and these funds are then used for the manufacturing process, for investment in new products and for payment to shareholders. In so doing the firms make a multitude of decisions which affect thousands of employees and innumerable individual suppliers.

The study uses sales revenue as its financial envelope and proceeds by computer analysis to show how the five different industries – mechanical engineering, electronics, motor vehicles and chemicals and textiles – in four separate countries – Japan, the United States, West Germany and the United Kingdom – spend this money both in times of prosperity and of decline. Studies are made of investment in research, innovation and fixed capital; of the growing expenditure on outside services; of taxes; and finally of interest rates and interest payments where money is borrowed. It is found that each technology has its own typical pattern of cash flow, which changes little over time.

For an industry to survive in the long term, current costs, investments and dividends must be funded primarily from total revenue. It follows that if the industry is to grow, sales receipts must grow. So the first important finding is that, in a free market, revenue must be maximised. This may be achieved by outstanding quality, good marketing or early delivery. In contrast, any extraneous influence that *reduces* the potential takings below that set by the discipline of the market is destructive. The evidence is that the premium earned on innovative products will be used to finance the next generation of research and product development and so ensure further growth.

Government, too, gains when industry maximises revenue. Acting as a tax collector, British manufacturing industry passes just under one fifth of its sales revenue to Government as national insurance and direct and indirect taxes. The German proportion is similar.

The analytical technique used in this survey involves the assembly of a mass of information that is compatible over a decade. From this information certain rules of thumb emerge regarding aggregate costs, employment costs and required levels of investment. These are discussed and compared across the four countries. A movement away from the norm is found to be useful as a diagnostic tool.

The provision of finance for investment appears to be a matter of great importance in most economic studies – and in practice it is largely self-generated. Money is raised on the market for running costs (short-term loans) or for investment (long-term loans) but even when equity is included the sums are small and interest payments and dividends are a small proportion of disbursements. Japan, however, proves to be the exception and companies depend on Japanese savings to a much greater extent.

The book also discusses the cultural and legislative influences in the four countries. These vary greatly and are important. The conclusion is that government intervention has many pitfalls. As a counter-inflationary device, the British attempt to control prices from 1945 to 1980 was a massive and expensive failure, bringing a loss of jobs and a fall in output in four of the five industries studied. In Germany Federal money was used with discretion to strengthen the perceived weakness in market intelligence and in research. The experience in the United States is quite different. Lack of confidence after the Japanese onslaught may have encouraged payments for outside expertise – to a point at which the level of current costs rose alarmingly. Finally in Japan, MITI's objective was to take an active part in market intelligence, but such planning has not prevented prices falling to a level which indicates strongly that capacity has become over-expanded.

An extensive literature in the disciplines of economics, management and sociology has concerned itself with manufacturing industry, its culture, its attitudes and its success or failure. Inevitably the outcome is qualitative and open to argument. But it need not be so. In practice it is possible to measure certain changes directly, as for example the impact of higher interest rates; do they increase costs or do they reduce borrowing? What effect does a rise in the minimum wage have on employment costs, or on employment? Again each of these topics has its own extensive literature, and bold claims are made as to the effect on costs. But in practice the manufacturer may escape the expected consequences by adopting an alternative policy.

A manufacturing enterprise is a highly complex and sensitive organism – with boundless options in its choice of markets, processes and product range. Furthermore, any one decision will cause ripples through the organisation, for money can be spent only once and loans are expensive to service. It follows that the final outcome of any one strategy cannot be described in qualitative terms alone, the facts must be observed over several cycles. How have costs reacted to exogenous change? Did the oil shock bring a temporary or a permanent increase in costs? How do Japanese methods of production and man-management affect their pattern of costs?

Fortunately for this 'supply-side' analysis the facts are available annually in the manufacturing census and in the revenue and other information published by European governments and by those of Japan and the United States. These publications report the pattern of costs, the funding of investment and the distribution to shareholders and proprietors. The study covers the period 1972 to 1985 with some earlier figures for Britain.

PART I

THE CONTEXT OF THE STUDY

1 Concepts and cost structures

This study is concerned with two distinct flows of cash, first with payments or disbursements made by manufacturers in the course of their manufacturing operations and sales (their costs of current output) and second with investment – the promotion of research, innovation and plant renewal (their costs for future output). These two bodies of cost, plus the distribution of any surplus income to working proprietors, shareholders, reserves, etc., are shown in relation to the sales revenue over the same period. The cash flow model, therefore, is concerned with the aggregate of decisions that result in actual disbursements (money out) compared with the aggregate of monies received for products sold or work done (money in).

This type of 'supply side' analysis, based on actual money flows year by year, differs markedly from the usual economic approach which is primarily concerned with physical output. To obtain an estimate of output, the accountants of companies must provide estimates of changes in the value of stocks of finished goods, work-in-progress and materials. Despite using generally accepted accounting methods, such estimates can be no more than educated guesses; for only at the point of sale can their true value be determined. It follows that by trying to convert figures of the value of annual sales – which reflect the market precisely – into figures of gross output the sensitivity of the observations can be lost. A precise economic variable has become 'funny money'.

The second difference arises from the recognition that, within a manufacturing company, there are two flows of cash and not one. The first set of expenses represents the purchases for shop-floor operations – those serving current output. The second set of expenses is concerned with future output, and this includes research, planning, design, product development, tooling, etc., plus the purchase of the plant and machinery required for new products or for renewal or expansion.

In this analysis the costs of current output are taken to be the aggregate disbursements for the factory and sales operations plus taxes and interest payments. The difference between the total of these costs and the value of sales is the disposable funds. In the very short term the costs of current output are immutable, in contrast to the disposable funds which (as the name implies) are discretionary and so subject to board decisions – for example how much shall be allocated for investment and how much for distribution to shareholders? Funds from other sources – interest received, money from foreign investments, sales of plant, subsidies etc – also make a contribution to the cash flow of the industry and are shown as 'other funds'.

This form of analysis is explained more fully, and illustrated diagramatically, in Appendix C.

2

Investment: the wider perspective

Disbursements that are made with the future output of the company in mind comprise tangible investment (buildings, plant and machinery) and the so-called intangible investment, which comprises research and development (primarily laboratory work), the commercialisation of research results (or innovation) and licensing[1].

Innovation comprises new product marketing and market intelligence, final product development and design engineering, tooling and industrial engineering and manufacturing start-up. It is described by one company in its annual report as[2]:

Creating new markets, strengthening shares in existing markets and increasing operational efficiency by the introduction of new technologies.

The first official study of the costs of technological innovation was undertaken by the Government of Canada in 1970 after discussions with industry[3]. Later, in West Germany, the costs in mechanical engineering were measured in 1976, 1980 and 1984 by the German Machinery and Plant Manufacturers Association (VDMA) in the course of their four-yearly assessment of all costs[4]. Surveys of expenditure have also been carried out by the IFO institute in Germany[5]. The present study has adopted the comprehensive definition of innovation used by Statistics Canada after consultations with industry[6].

Although intangible investment may appear to have disparate features (encompassing commercial as well as scientific skills) it is, in fact, a continuum as all the activities listed involve resources that are allocated for the same objective, the introduction of new or improved products.

The differences observed in the resources allocated for research and innovation lie in company strategy, and in the all-important level and type of staffing. If a company purchases a complete manufacturing system, it is buying the new technology embodied in the plant and its instruction manual – and a minimum number of trained staff are needed to start up and maintain the industrial process. At the other end of the spectrum the research, design and development of the product or process will be undertaken within the company with its own specialist staff. So what are the respective benefits and the disadvantages? It can be argued that the purchase of a complete plant involves 'minimum risk'; but this strategy has its own dangers. The market may change and a company that lacks qualified staff is 'locked-in' and unable to modify or update its plant. In contrast the firm that has maintained its own team of scientists, engineers and designers is flexible and can keep up with changing techniques and changing customer needs. Later, we shall see how Britain has tended to favour the first strategy, and Germany and Japan the second – with consequential differences in the levels of qualified staff.

The traditional use of expenditure on fixed assets to denote 'investment' is deficient in two respects – the plant may be leased rather than purchased and, second, new technology may be obtained on licence. It follows that companies can choose from a range of alternatives. At one extreme is the purchase of a tried and tested plant which may already be out of date; at the other is the employment of an in-house team of engineers and designers who can modify existing plant as necessary, while designing and developing more advanced plant to keep up with changing technologies and market needs. Yet another alternative is to use contract research laboratories. In practice large firms are known to use all these procedures from time to time, for few firms have all the relevant knowledge and expertise within their own technical staff.

3

The theory of innovation

There has been an immense effort in recent years to find a theory of innovation – an effort that has been described by Richard Nelson as part of their 'differential productivity growth puzzle'[7]. The problem seems to be that theoretical economics see manufacturing as a single operation – merely supply responding to demand – whereas, in practice, entrepreneurs must play a double role. First, their manufacturing operation must be efficient, that is, within the current technology they must produce and market an acceptable and reliable product: second, they have to advance their technology and plan their future range of products to ensure the survival of their company.

The conventions of accountancy tend to blur this vital distinction by treating all disbursements for research and innovation as an 'overhead'. It follows that the vital blending of new technological and marketing skills – essential to review the product range and maintain competitiveness – is given a label with derogatory connotation.

In markets that are worldwide, a product range requires continuous updating. Furthermore, the economic skills of market intelligence and planning are as essential as the technological skills; the customer must be satisfied in terms of relevance as well as quality.

Thus activities to ensure future sales, both in quality and quantity, must be continuous; and they must have a specific budget equal in its effectiveness to that of competitors. The cost of failing to provide finance for adequate planning, market research and technical effort is the loss of customers and so the reduction of revenue; and if this continues the company will cease to trade. In short, innovation must be seen as the economic imperative and it must be given a budget, the size of which is relevant to the technology and the speed of technological advances. The newer the technology, the higher the sum that must be spent.

To summarise, a theory of innovation must recognise two parallel flows of cash, one for manufacturing and sales and one for tangible and intangible investment. Within these two flows are the individual items of cost, the mix in both cases being unique to the technology. This implies a normal business environment; but in the real world expectations can be upset by exogenous influences and changes in the cost structure record these disturbances, in both direction and magnitude (Tables C1 to C20, pp.135-154)).

Such changes in the patterns of cost provide a first-time indicator of potential change, which may be positive or negative. Annual statements of revenue and costs, when assembled, enable turning points to be detected and used as evidence of recovery or warnings of progressive decline. These indicators will be reported in the industrial studies that follow, related both to world events and to the industrial culture within which the industry is operating.

The pattern of costs in growth and decline

Guidelines or rules of thumb, designed for the assessment of manufacturing performance, have presented themselves in the course of historical analyses of costs; they are totally empirical. However, as in matters of housekeeping, rules of thumb have a strong basis of common sense. For example, no organisation could survive if it paid 99 per cent of its takings to its employees. But if that is absurd, as it is, how much would be prudent? How generous can a company be to its staff without damaging its future viability?

From observations of patterns of costs going back to 1972 (1963 in the case of the United Kingdom) it has proved possible to suggest a normal cost structure for each technology, one where revenue meets all current costs of manufacture while funding an investment programme sufficient to keep the industry up to date and its products competitive. The suggested normal pattern of costs in the five industries of the study, expressed in percentages of the value of sales, is as follows:

	Electronics	Chemicals	Motor vehicles	Mechanical engineering	Textiles
For current output	74	85	84	86	94
Materials	38	50	50	40	50
Employment	25	20	22	32	25
Industrial services	3	2	2	4	4
Other services	2	8	6	6	9
Interest payments	2	2	2	2	2
Taxes	4	3	2	2	4
Disposable funds	26	15	16	14	6
Other funds	6	5	8	4	4
Available funds	32	20	24	18	10
For investment	20	14	12	10	6
R&D and innovation	15	9	8	6	2
Fixed capital	5	5	4	4	4
Surplus/deficit	12	6	12	8	4
Value added	57	40	42	50	37

The concept here is of a 'balanced cost structure'. Thus when one or more of the costs shows a movement away from such a norm, this observation becomes a first-line indicator of change – there may be growth potential because lower costs of manufacture are leaving more cash for investment, or there may be a danger of decline when higher costs of manufacture attenuate funds for investment.

For the five industries studied here, investment in R&D and innovation is highest in the industry with the newest technology (electronics) and lowest in the industry with the oldest (textiles). In contrast, investment in fixed capital is of the same order (4 to 5 per cent) in all five industries.

However, there can be alternative ways of achieving the same results, as, for example, Japan's use of contract services to supplement a smaller in-house staff. The use of the normal cost structure as a reference point enables the extent of the diversion to be measured. (See Tables C8, p.142 and C16, p.150).

The relative movement of input and output prices has also proved to be a valuable diagnostic tool. With a competitive product in a free market, increases in producer prices reflect improving quality and so can be expected to move slightly ahead of prices of material inputs (to allow a rising added value). But if the situation is reversed, with producer prices lagging behind material prices, then this can indicate one of three things:

• price control
• falling demand prompting discounted prices
• dumping[8].

In interpreting the analysis of cost structures, it should be remembered that, if revenue is depressed for any reason, then material costs will appear as a higher proportion. Similarly, unless there is an offsetting cost reduction, total costs rise as a proportion of the value of sales and disposable funds fall.

The question of time-lag should also be considered. Supposing price control is removed with the result that sales revenue rises, labour becomes more co-operative and the cost structure comes into balance. Does output show immediate improvement? Economic logic suggests that this would be unlikely as the damage would have been cumulative; investment would have been reduced and product development slowed down. The analyses of the data show that two to three years are needed before markets are regained. For instance, British mechanical engineering, effectively freed from price control in May 1979, brought its cost structure into balance in 1981; but did not resume a rising trend of output until 1985. This type of analysis can be a useful tool when making projections of future performance or of employment.

2 Competitiveness: alternative concepts

Collins English Dictionary defines 'competitiveness' as, 'sufficiently low in price or high in quality to be successful against commercial rivals'. If we are concerned solely with sales of the product (or range of products) and with the achievement of a larger market share, this definition is sufficient. But the concept can also embrace the idea of long-term economic performance and company survival. From this base, how do we define a competitive company or industry? If a company is gaining market share by under-pricing, is it still 'competitive'? Can a company be considered 'competitive' if its financial viability is dependent on interest received from investments made outside the company in earlier years? A further issue concerns long-term strategies. If a company is gaining market share by selling so cheaply that it cannot afford to do adequate research or product development, would we consider this an acceptable strategy? These strategies will be examined in greater detail using official data as evidence.

Quality versus quantity
The dictionary definition of competitiveness underlines the essential dichotomy in the marketing strategy of a product. Does a firm maintain the demand for its product by outstanding quality or does it market a run-of-the-mill product at a price below that of its rivals?

The cost analyses presented in Part II provide some of the evidence required to solve this dilemma. Furthermore, our four countries exhibit the results of four different approaches to world markets. The belief that German companies lean towards competitiveness through quality is borne out, and the analysis of cash flow shows how the extra costs are borne. British industry, historically preoccupied with costs, has until recently gone for quantity, under the precept 'high volume low margin'. Japan has used both, high quality combined with prices that are low with respect to costs – a strategy that has brought a growing market share but high dependence on domestic savers, even to the point of financial instability and dependence on the 'zaitech' financial management strategy. Companies in the United States have maintained quality and so a high gross margin on the shop floor but, nevertheless, have a high-cost operation because of massive expenditure on external services. However, their high-cost production is partially offset by non-trading income – primarily income from earlier investments.

High market share, therefore, can be achieved by three routes:
- by producing quality products in a specialist area where margins are high enough to fund substantial R&D and innovation

- by taking a risk on future viability, (cutting R&D and innovation) to be competitive in price
- by internal subsidisation, whereby inadequate disposable funds are augmented by the income from past investments or merchanting.

Falling market share is inevitable if companies are trapped in a downward spiral. The evidence suggests that such a downward spiral afflicted British industry from 1945 to 1979. The prices permitted by the Price Commission[9] reduced margins (particularly for innovative products) and put excessive emphasis on reducing costs while restrictive practices were tending to raise them. Government policies, including tax credits, were another influence persuading companies to buy fixed assets, leaving even less of their disposable funds for R&D and innovation. As products became less competitive, output fell and margins fell further.

So the questions to be answered are: 'Is competitiveness a single or a double concept? Are firms to be considered competitive if, in raising market share, they discount their prices, are unable to fund investment without subsidies and so become financially unstable?'

Why exports?

Seen as an indicator of performance, exports and market share appear all-important. Yet it is clear from the flow of funds analysis that if an industry is to have a future it must maximise sales revenue – irrespective of its origin.The Government sees this rather differently; exports earn foreign exchange – a major element in the balance of payments.

There are, however, two reasons why firms try to export on their own behalf – despite the difficulties encountered with language, labelling, and representation abroad:

- the home market may be too small to use manufacturing capacity fully
- export markets help to flatten out swings in home demand.

While Japan more than doubled the volume of output of motor vehicles between 1970 and 1986 (and market share rose from 9 to 29 per cent), this was achieved by combining quality with competitive prices – reflecting its need to break into new world markets and to earn foreign exchange.

3 Money in and money out: the options

In the cash flow model which underpins the analysis of industrial performance we are concerned with the aggregate of decisions leading to actual disbursements of cash (money out)compared with the aggregate value of cheques received for the products in that same year (money in). In the computer analysis (Appendix B) it will be noted that receipts from sales are augmented by a number of smaller sums, which include interest receipts, sales of discarded plant and new investment funds from overseas. Also, but in a different category, there are any sums borrowed. The miscellaneous receipts, listed under 'other funds', add from 5 to 10 per cent to the sales value. The amount borrowed can be measured either in terms of outstanding debt or as payments of interest.

It is helpful at this point to restate the fundamentals of resource allocation within any manufacturing company. Disbursements must be made for current output, that is, to ensure deliveries to customers, and a separate flow of cash is required for investment, that is, for future output – which must include market intelligence, research, design, tooling and fixed assets. Finally, funds must be available to reward working proprietors, directors and shareholders. Within the parameters set by the sales revenue the decisions made regarding these three flows are of the utmost importance.

Figure 1 (p.29) presents the four areas of cash flow studied in the model.

Short-term and long-term: current attitudes
The conceptual approach summarised in Figure 1 demonstrates that entrepreneurs must decide their future policy on the basis of the money available to them from revenue or, more precisely, the expected revenue of the forthcoming year. Although a bank overdraft or receipts from issues of share and loan capital provide some flexibility, essentially the entrepreneur is operating within a closed loop.

It will be noted that, in the very short term, the disbursements for current output are fixed, thus there is discretion only over the residual or 'disposable funds'. The decisions made here are fundamental, for they decide two things – the financial standing of the company in world stock markets and the strength of its future economic performance. So, the important questions are, How much of this sum should be allocated to investment? How much should be paid out to shareholders? Put to reserves? Put another way, should financial strength be sought by paying higher dividends to avoid takeovers or should the emphasis be on finance for research and innovation so that the product range can be continuously updated by a strong technical team?

It is clear that decision making at this juncture is strongly influenced by the financial culture of the country concerned and the ownership of industrial companies[10]. In a financial climate that looks for high share values to avoid takeovers it may be all important to maintain the dividend, whereas in other countries (for example Germany and Japan) the company and its bank manager may decide that funds should be diverted from dividends to improve the quality of the product range.

Christopher Lorenz, in his monograph *Investing in Success*, explained the situation as follows[11]:

> We have now reached the crux of the matter. Whereas German banks are geared to the long term, British stockbrokers take an almost entirely short-term view of company prospects, focussed on the next few profit declarations and dividend payout. In their eyes, a successful company is one whose profits and dividends are likely to increase over the next six months, year or (at most) two years.

In this context the figures in Table 1 (p.30) are interesting – they show that the proportion of 'available funds' allocated to investment is highest in West Germany and Japan.

Ten years ago, when Lorenz was writing on the subject, there was little or no understanding of the problem or of its significance. Now it is becoming an issue of some interest and an international study of how companies are financed has been initiated by the Centre for Economic Policy Research. Furthermore, economic commentators have recognised the influence of the financial climate on the economic strategy of industry; for example, Anthony Harris, *Financial Times*, 18 June 1987, wrote of the support given by banks to company directors in West Germany:

> The crucial reason is that he will enjoy – or if he is inefficient, he will suffer – a committed, supportive long-term relationship with the bank. This means that the risk of takeover— the ultimate loss of control – are minimal.

Of our four countries, the United Kingdom and the United States have industries whose futures are influenced by the money markets where current judgments are seen as essentially short term, while in the other two, West Germany and Japan, industry relies more on a banking system which is geared to assist longer-term projects.

Short-term: the United Kingdom and the United States

In Britain and the United States, the price earnings ratios of enterprises are closely watched by their shareholders and the financial institutions and, in consequence, resource allocation tends to be influenced by short-term financial considerations. An American observer sums up this type of situation succinctly[12]:

> Companies have cut back on research and capital spending to maximise short-term profits and ward off the raiders. That rips right into the heart of America's competitiveness.

We see the evidence of this pressure in the cost structures. In Britain, for instance, funds for investment and distribution tend to be given equal weight so that, if costs rise such that disposable funds are squeezed, then funds for R&D and innovation are reduced to maintain dividends (see Table 1, p.30).

However, there is one exception. Probably because it consists of large firms, the motor vehicle industry in the United States adopted the longer-term view. In 1980 it pushed R&D and innovation above the level of West Germany and Japan and accepted the consequent high interest payments in 1981 and 1982 of up to 7 per cent of sales value. As a result it is now challenging Japan and has a similar rate of growth. This proves that in certain situations – in this case the challenge of Japanese technology and market intelligence – the broad pattern of behaviour can be altered. However, the British industry, despite considerable government assistance, has restructured its operations but at a level 30 per cent below that of 1970.

While industries in Britain and the United States both operate in the goldfish bowl environment of the City and the Stock Exchange, the limitations have proved to be more serious in the United Kingdom. In all five industries, growth has been lowest in the United Kingdom; the problems engendered by price control, devaluation and restrictive practices, have been exacerbated by the inflexibility of City financing. Companies in the United States have, to a large extent, been permitted a more flexible strategy and, while one detected a state of complacency in the early 1970s, the competition from Japan (both in Japan and in the United States) has been effective in creating a renewed challenge.

In general, the United States suffered steep but temporary falls in output and R&D but maintained throughout a reasonable base level of product development. In contrast the financial straitjacket brought a heavy reduction in research in the United Kingdom – an outcome for which the City and successive Governments, with their persistent price control until the end of the 1970s, must share the blame.

If any moral can be drawn from this evidence, it is that short-termism, can be detrimental to growth and so to employment. Influences that persuade enterprises to channel available funds to shareholders rather than to technologists and designers run the risk of losing customers and sales revenue, which can in turn threaten jobs.

Longer-term: West Germany and Japan

The second pair, Japan and West Germany, have three things in common – high costs, the absence of City pressure and governments that pursue consistent and logical policies. In other respects, particularly in their pricing policies, they are different.

Germany, with a history of technological excellence, and a watchful but essentially non-interventionist Government, had a headstart on Japan. R&D and innovation in German industry have been maintained as a top priority and the funding has always equalled that of Japan, even where high manufacturing costs have made it impossible to fund this totally from sales receipts. It should be noted that the high costs of manufacturing have arisen primarily because payments to employees were well above the norm. While these high payments were thought appropriate as the employees' share in the economic miracle, such high rewards, plus substantial R&D and innovation, could not be achieved without borrowed funds. This situation is under the control of enterprises, however, and, with the gradual diminution of employment costs in relation to total costs, balance in the cost structure is returning.

A different reason explains the high costs in Japanese industry. Employment costs here are closely controlled (as low as a third of those in West Germany); but costs of materials, being largely imported, are out of Japanese control. And a further constraint on margins is the so-called export offensive from South Korea and Taiwan.

Unlike the manufacturing environments of the United States, West Germany and the United Kingdom which have developed slowly, the Japanese system has been planned in detail to take into account the full requirements of a population of 120 million in a small island with few natural resources. To raise the standard of living, the growth of output and market share became the first priority. To achieve this, Japan used its one national resource

– highly educated manpower that fully understood the economic realities. With a national consensus and with no deep political divisions, restrictive practices or complacency, the planned growth was under way from 1950. Despite the oil price shock, by 1974 Japan was rapidly taking over markets from France, Germany, United Kingdom and the United States (Table A1, p.124)).

Growth has been outstanding; but as competition increased a weakness has developed in the prices received. Since 1972 output prices have failed to match prices of materials and a situation has developed in which the total revenue is too small to cover costs of current output and investment. It follows that the difference is met by extensive borrowing, the so-called 'aggressive financing', which has made possible the doubling of output since 1970. Furthermore, Japanese companies have been speculating on the Tokyo stock market to make up for falling industrial profits[13].

In the financial climate of Japan, the use of loan funds to assist manufacturing sales is acceptable to savers who are content with minimal dividends. Highly competitive prices have given Japanese industry the highest market share; nevertheless, the industries are vulnerable. Competition is coming from South Korea, Taiwan and, increasingly, from the United States. There is no room to cut prices further and, already, there is some reduction in the scale of R&D reported.

To summarise, of all four countries, two, Britain and the United States, raise money in a City short-term environment and so must always operate to preserve the value of shares. In contrast, industries in West Germany and Japan can raise money through the banks who, speaking generally, are prepared to take a longer-term view where money is needed for research and product development.

Getting the work done: the service revolution

In the last 20 years or so there has been a silent revolution in the management and payment of the industrial task force.In mechanical engineering in Britain in 1968, about 6 per cent of sales revenue was disbursed for a portfolio of contracted services, rising to 11 per cent in 1984. These services include work done on materials given out, repairs and maintenance, commercial insurance, mail, telephones, telex etc, advertising and professional services. Moreover, in some industries, the total costs of these services exceeded those of in-house employees. In the chemical industry in the USA in 1984, payments for services were higher than employment costs by a substantial amount; in Japan they were more than twice as high. This surprising result is also one element in their high manufacturing costs.

Japanese information does not give full details of the composition of this figure for services. But it is estimated from British data that charges for administrative services (postage, telephones, etc) are about 1 per cent of sales value. In Japan prices have been raised only for mail, a 30 per cent increase since 1980, so the increase recorded must have been spent on professional services, insurance and transport. It has been suggested that hiring specialists is more economical than employing them as full-time staff[14], but the evidence throws some doubt on this. As appointments of specialists are decided by management or by the commercial department rather than by the personnel department, company directors may not be aware of the costs that they are incurring (Table 2, p.30).

An interesting sideline for the statistician is the effect of these management changes on the index of productivity – that is, the index of output divided by the index of labour input. If company employees are being supplanted by non-company employees, that is, by outside workers and consultants, then the apparent increases in output per head could be spurious.

Certainly it would not necessarily imply any improvement in economic performance, but it might well be the reverse.

Interest rates and interest payments

One of the most frequently discussed economic variables is the rate of interest. In practice each country reports a number of rates which reflect both the type of loan and the length of time a loan is required. Short-term loans (including bank overdrafts) tend to command a lower rate of interest than longer-term loans, but, where the information is available, they seem to be the more important.

Central Bank discount rates reflect the interest paid on longer-term loans. However, in terms of payments made, those on short-term loans are larger so it is to be expected that the average rate of interest paid by industry will be slightly lower than the discount rate. Prior to the recession of 1971, discount rates lay between 3 and 8 per cent. Table 3 (p.31)shows that in 1987 the highest rate was in the United Kingdom and the lowest in Japan. See also Figure 2 (p.31)covering a longer period.

Interest payments as a percentage of sales revenue show considerable variation (Table 4, p.32). Despite having the highest discount rates, interest payments as a percentage of sales are among the lowest in the United Kingdom. This reflects the low borrowing regime practised in British industry – the United Kingdom being broadly 'market-based' with highly active securities markets, dominated by institutional investors. Equity ratios in 1980 were 46 per cent in the UK compared with 27 per cent in West Germany and 21 per cent in Japan[15]. In consequence, resources distributed as dividends in the UK are higher than in Japan (Table 5, p.32).

4 Remuneration and employment

Keynes in the *General Theory* reminds us that:

> The amount of employment, both in each individual firm and industry and in the aggregate depends on the amount of the proceeds which the entrepreneurs expect to receive from the corresponding output[16].

Since the *General Theory* was published in 1936, Keynes' assumptions as to the dynamics of employment can be checked against the evidence from the annual census of production in each of the four countries. His observation that the demand for labour is expressed in money values is amply borne out. In the absence of strong exogenous pressures, it is found that the proportion of sales receipts (or sale-proceeds) allocated to employment for current output is oddly consistent over time. To illustrate this finding, employment costs in mechanical engineering in the United Kingdom and the United States over the last decade were found to be 31-32 per cent of sales revenue (Table 6, p.32).

This consistency in decision making implies a number of economic relationships that are very important:

- the pool of money available for employees for current output – the employment budget – is directly related to sales receipts – and so rises and falls with it;
- since national insurance, pension funds etc. (the social costs) come within the employment budget, a rise in these demands can reduce the cash available for paying to employees;
- the allocation of cash to the employment budget is under the control of the entrepreneur. The consistency suggests that, with trial and error, he has recognised a prudent proportion for his particular enterprise which then averages out at a constant figure for the industry as a whole.

These facts give credence to the two linked observations made by Keynes that the demand for labour is expressed in money values and that this decision depends on the amount of the proceeds which the entrepreneurs expect to receive. But while, for any given value of sales, an estimate can be made of the expenditure on employment for current output, no such estimate can be made of the numbers employed, for that number depends on the cost per employee (wages and salaries plus social charges). This logic is illustrated in Figure 3 (p.33).

Much has been written regarding the way that wages are determined, especially in periods of growth and of recession, but the most influential change in recent history – that from company bargaining to centralised wage bargaining – has been little discussed. When wages were decided primarily on the basis of individual company performance, a general rise in wages was unlikely unless there had been a substantial increase in the value of sales. As a result, wages in less successful firms might fall behind those in more successful firms but there need be no change in the number employed. Furthermore, in the absence of union pressure this might not be commented upon, nor even known outside the company.

Evidence from the Census of Production in the United Kingdom reflects the situation that arose in 1974 when the Social Contract formalised centralised wage fixing and brought general awareness of negotiated wage levels. Many companies had to pay increases that were substantially higher than the increases they expected in sales revenue and, to quote the economists at the OECD, a process of 'wage adjustment' ensued. Other companies went into liquidation[17]. In other words, while the employment budget maintained its relationship with sales-proceeds, the number of employees that could be supported at the new higher level of remuneration had to fall. At the same time, with the more advanced technology becoming available, such reductions of staff were manageable without reducing the level of output.

Table 6 shows employment costs in mechanical engineering in relation to sales and to the other costs. Despite the rise in output until 1974, the steep fall and subsequent recovery, employment costs as a percentage of sales value have been virtually unchanged over 20 years. This implies that the number of people sharing the employment budget becomes a variable dictated by social choice rather than by economic expectations. As a corollary, if the number employed is a social rather than an economic variable, then the index of labour productivity is likewise governed by social choice rather than by economics. This may help to explain Richard Nelson's 'differential productivity growth puzzle'[18].

The proportions in Table 6 (p.32) show that employment costs took 32 per cent of sales and that this proportion was virtually unchanged in the United Kingdom. The position in the United States was similar. Nevertheless, cultural pressures for conformity can overwhelm economic judgement. In West Germany under the regime of Concerted Action, employers felt morally obliged to pay the recommended national increases, even if the expected level of sales did not justify this. In consequence, employment costs rose to 36 per cent in 1975 and 1977 and overall costs to 94 per cent (Table C2, p.136). But, as intangible investment was seen as all-important, external funding was necessary and this included a government subsidy and bank loans. While the negotiating consensus in West Germany became a way of raising employment costs, the Japanese used a different procedure altogether – a procedure for lowering employment costs.

In Japan permanent staff can make up as little as a third of all the work force; the remainder are part-time or employed on short-term contracts. Thus the Japanese mechanical engineering industry reports employment costs (including the smaller social costs) as low as 18 per cent (Table C4, p.138). In this situation, where work is organised under a different system, comparisons must be made with caution. However, if the costs of contract work are included, the broad aggregates are comparable. This comparison shows that, before patterns of costs are compared, it is essential to understand the underlying cultural and management basis.

However, while Japan has operated this three-tiered employment system for many years, other countries seem to be moving in the same direction. Tasks, previously done within the company, are increasingly performed by outsiders. The reasons for this are various, but must include:

• more generous redundancy terms
• increased complexity of technology such that a wider range of expertise is needed

• greater flexibility in the number of staff used.

While it is generally believed that this procedure is less costly than employing experts as full-time staff, data from the census and revenue authorities in West Germany and the United States throw doubt on this assumption. Higher bills for outside expertise are recorded but they are not associated with an equivalent reduction in the cost of full-time staff. In consequence, a high-cost manufacture results (see Table C3, p.137 for the United States).

5 Indicators of performance

The assembly of all the relevant data in a cash flow model provides a useful diagnostic tool. It can analyse low achievement and can make an assessment of the prospects of renewed growth and financial viability. To make such assessments, all the data are needed (60 separate variables) but it is also useful in the first instance to study a series of indicators, particularly when making international comparisons. Those suggested are as follows:
* the index of output
* foreign trade and market share
* value added
* spending on new technology
* financial indicators

The index of output
The index of output represents the volume of output – thus giving prominence to physical output as opposed to financial strength. Even though a rise in output would be expected to reflect an improved financial situation, this is not necessarily so. As has been seen, for instance with the textile and motor-vehicle industries, government regulations can and do sever the link between output and financial viability. Furthermore, a policy of increasing output to ensure a growing market share may imply discounted prices and so a measure of financial risk. Index numbers for four of the five industries are shown in Table 52 (p.119).

Foreign trade and market share
The amount of a product that is exported, and the proportion of the sales of the industry that this implies, is a more sensitive indicator. Rising exports indicate that the products are judged to be equivalent to, or better than, products from other countries. A fall in exports can suggest either that quality has failed to keep up with equivalent foreign products or, alternatively, that companies are too busy with their home market to trouble to enter the more difficult foreign markets.

Value added
Value added as a percentage of sales is a useful indicator of the performance of an industry, allowing as it does for costs of administrative services and outside specialists. It is clear from Table 7 (p.34) that the Japanese industry is out of line in each of the five industries; for example, value added in mechanical engineering is 16 points lower than in the UK and the USA. This low figure is explained by the low prices obtained for Japanese products in

a highly competitive market, the high costs (relative to sales value) of their material inputs, and their dependence on extra-mural services. It raises some doubts as to the value of this indicator in that, to some extent, services are becoming an alternative to employment, rather than a purchase in the normal sense.

Spending on new technology

Spending on new technology or investment covers a spectrum of activities from research at one end to the installation of new capital equipment at the other. Two aspects of spending on technology provide sensitive indicators of the health of an industry, the total level of expenditure and the proportion of intangible investment, and the manpower involved.

In the five industries studied, each has an expected or normal level of expenditure on new technology, and this reflects the age of the technology in use. The new and rapidly advancing technologies require the highest allocation of resources; the most traditional the lowest. Thus a normal level in electronics is 20 per cent of the value of sales, chemicals 14 per cent, motor vehicles 12 per cent, mechanical engineering 10 per cent and textiles 6 per cent.

To maintain competitiveness the industry must have a team of senior technologists and supporting staff, whose job is to research, design and develop new products, to modify processes and to maintain relevance and quality as customers' needs change. This implies that a substantial proportion of investment spending, over half, must be on intangible investment. Empirical observations on required spending or 'norms' will be discussed in the chapters describing each industry.

Financial indicators

Economic indicators can reflect two very different aspects of performance: first, the financial success (or otherwise) of a particular industry on its own account and, second, the contribution made by the industry to the gross domestic product and the balance of payments. These will not necessarily coincide; an example can be drawn from the mechanical engineering industry in Japan where rapidly increasing exports were achieved by offering high quality products at prices that did not cover costs. The foreign exchange earned from the high market share was, however, of advantage to the balance of payments, in that it helped to finance essential imports.

So far, we have discussed indicators of performance that reflect the internal working of the industry. However, this omits the interests of the owners, the stockholders. Thus the decisions made by the board of directors must take into account the impact that the announcement of the annual dividend may have on the share price and so on the attitude of the bank. The level of dividends is not, therefore, an objective indicator of performance; it reflects the judgement of the company board and the market conditions.

Little research has been done on the amount of influence that the City has on company decision making, and in particular on the allocation of funds for research and innovation [19]. It is open to question whether some of the City indicators, such as the price/earnings ratio are worth studying. In practice, while such indicators are of importance on a day by day basis, they are too volatile to have lasting value and, when examined historically, appear to bear no relation to the hard facts of performance. To determine, in retrospect, whether market valuations have had a significant influence, there is no alternative but to study the financial pages for the days in question. In a stable situation, the influence of such daily indicators is marginal, but in a crisis situation, when they affect share dealings on a larger scale, they may signal the difference between the life and death of a company: a merger or its continuing independence.

6 The cash flow models

All of the main series of data presented for each of the four countries are from published sources, their origin being primarily government departments of finance, industry and technology, central banks and taxation authorities. The materials as originally published is very detailed, so it has been possible to rearrange the data for the four countries so that they are, to a high degree, on a comparable basis.

Of course one will always get some minor deviations in the coverage of data from country to country which derives from national peculiarities ind efinitions, collection practice, data processing and the like. But this is a general problem of all international comparisons. As this study mostly concentrates on typical patterns over time and not on a comparison of absolute figures, these smaller differences do not really affect its findings. The measurements of revenue and costs are assembled to become part of the same system of annual cash flow.

The VDMA surveys of mechanical engineering in 1976, 1980 and 1984 indicate a rise in research and innovation costs as a percentage of sales value. This is consistent with the introduction of complex systems into a traditional industry and so is reflected in the estimates for this industry. The assessments for the other four industries of the costs of innovation use the early Canadian studies, and the more recent German surveys carried out by the IFO institute in Munich. While it cannot be claimed that the costings revealed by these small samples of companies are representative of the industry as a whole, they are used, pro term, as an acceptable surrogate.

Estimates of expenditure
In preparing the estimates of expenditure on innovation two further assumptions were made:
- first that the translation of R&D knowledge into a new product via the innovation phase would have the same technical characteristics across country boundaries, and therefore the same, or very similar, cost characteristics;
- second that companies in each industry which were not undertaking R&D would, on average, be spending on innovation the same proportion of sales receipts as the companies engaged in R&D.

The details of the analysis and the relationships for mechanical engineering in West Germany are shown in Appendix B. In this instance, the costings of research and innovation are taken from the VDMA survey for 1984.

7 The industrial and financial culture

Compared with the factual observations discussed in this study so far, matters of culture are elusive and difficult to pin down. Nevertheless cultural differences exist and there is evidence that they can and do influence industrial performance. The question must therefore be asked: Why, when companies in Western countries operate in the same markets and with similar financial services, should they be influenced by cultural differences?

The industrial culture of a country – broadly, its attitude to finance, employee welfare and technological change – impinges on industry in two ways, through legislation and through its own decision-making. The effects of legislation are direct and can be identified with reasonable precision – but the effects of culture on company decision-making are indirect and invisible and can be assessed only through observed differences in the allocation of resources.

Economic theory oversimplifies the matter of decision making. In the *General Theory*, Keynes was realistic[20]. He emphasised that entrepreneurial decisions are made 'in the light of the current expectations of prospective costs and sale-proceeds'. Thus because entrepreneurs in different countries are dealing with *expectations* rather than with hard facts, there is room for different judgments and so for varying decisions on the distribution of resources, on pricing and on investment. It is at this point – the handling uncertainties – that cultural differences can have a distinct influence. One such difference has already been is discussed and illustrated in Table 1 (p.30) – the different proportions of available funds devoted to tangible and intangible investment.

The entrepreneur must also take account of legislation and, in this, he meets his national culture at second hand. He may be instructed how to price his goods, how to reward his staff and how to plan his investment – or none of these things. The study will take account of such interventionist policies – how they reflect the national culture, how wide is their influence and what are the effects on the pattern of costs and so on.

West Germany

To understand the emergence of the unique industrial and financial culture of West Germany, a study of the history is important. Dr Yao-Su Hu, in his study of industrial banking[21], describes the difference in German, French and British attitudes to manufacturing in the context of both the timing of the Industrial Revolution and the philosophy of the time. He explains:

> Industrial banking arose on the continent of Europe in the middle of the 19th century, in response to the necessities of the time and in an attempt, conscious or perhaps

semi-conscious, to catch up with the lead that Britain had gained by undergoing the first Industrial Revolution in the world. I would add, however, the fact that industrialisation, and more generally economic development, were a more conscious and deliberate effort than in Britain. This is illustrated in the field of education. Napoleon had founded the famous École Polytechnique in 1794, and the Prussian government had established the Technische Hochschulen, long before official backing of engineering education took shape in England. Philosophers, national governments and ruling elites see industry as critical to national wealth and power (p.10).

Dr Hu also explores the origin of the industrial banks, and how they differed from the more traditional banks (p. 14):

> The great bankers, of the Rothschild type, were busy with the financial needs of the more important governments and, in general, the traditional banks were too conservative and fearful of risking their reputations. Thus, a new type of financial intermediary was needed, which would tap the savings of the nation (rather than just the personal fortunes of the wealthy) and make them available to industry in a suitable form.

But the association between the new generation of banks and industry was not merely through long-term lending, important though this was, especially at critical times. The banks also shared in the equity of many enterprises, and provided assistance in the underwriting and floating of new securities, of which they normally kept a part. Moreover, they generally assumed responsibility for the enterprises that they had promoted, and played an important role in providing technical advice and managerial talent.

West Germany has traditionally excelled in science and technology, but its current industrial and technological strength has its roots in the period of reconstruction following the end of the Second World War. The urgent need to rebuild the devastated industrial base left no room for the diversion of resources for idealistic welfare policies. Furthermore the difficulties of the situation led to close collaboration between banks, employers and unions and a full understanding on all sides of the need for high-value-added products, especially to rebuild the export trade.

The concentration on the essential task of rebuilding industry and the readiness to adopt new technologies meant that, by 1967, German industry had sufficient funds to undertake a second stage of renewal of its capital assets.

Thus the situation following the war had two effects. It reinforced the West German industrial and technological culture – that is, the combined effort of employees, unions and employers to produce goods of excellent quality – and, since this effort to rebuild industry required all available resources, the Federal Government was not tempted to indulge in ambitious schemes for public housing, hospitals and schools. Later, when industry could spare the funds for these desirable objectives, such schemes went ahead.

The German culture, and its system of industrial banking, limits direct government intervention. As explained by a senior government official, 'Civil servants do not understand industry; our role therefore is to identify the obstacles in the way of success and to do our best to remove them'. As will be described later, when the Federal Government did get involved – under the scheme of Concerted Action – damage was done to the pattern of costs which was not corrected until 1983.

Japan

The parallel with the German situation is close; the difference lay in the absence of a modern industrial background. In 1945 Japan had had little experience of competitive manufacture nor of the use of advanced technology for civil purposes. This had to be built up and the technology acquired. Nevertheless, with a population of 120 million in an island that is two thirds mountain and with few natural resources, industrial advance had to be rapid so that exportable goods could be produced to pay for the essential material imports. With no false pride, initial processes and technologies were obtained on licence from the United States and Europe. As described by a Japanese professor, 'Japanese industry is like a spinning top; if it stops spinning, the nation will starve. Our unions, our employers and our Government all understand this.'

Thus, as in West Germany, a pragmatic industrial culture was a necessity and this was well understood. The lack of technological experience, however, led to a considerable degree of government intervention in the early years – mainly with respect to research into overseas markets and the identification of the special product areas on which to concentrate. As in West Germany, the emerging industrial philosophy recognised that, while breaking into established markets, the maintenance of quality was all-important.

United Kingdom

The history of British manufacturing industry is very different. Again Dr Hu explains the contrasting features:

> The fact that Britain was the first nation to industrialise meant that industrial enterprises were started on a small scale and often on a family basis ... Successful businesses, who were spared the worries of organised international competition and who could thus afford to grow at their own pace, grew by ploughing back earnings. Thanks to Britain's industrial lead, profits were in all probability high, and the lack of international competition meant that there was no need to invest massively simply to remain competitive. This is the origin of the practice of relying almost entirely on internal finance to cover fixed capital expenditure, which has persisted until today (p.10).

So, in contrast to the situation in Germany and Japan, where manufacturing industry is recognised as the power-house of the economy and is treated accordingly, in Britain manufacturers are less well understood. Dr Hu suggests why this situation has arisen:

> Because of the natural, almost accidental, way in which industrialisation took place, it was almost taken for granted. There was little conscious self-reflection; the importance of industry to national wealth and power, and the possibility of promoting industrial development through deliberate and concerted measures of national policy, were (and probably still are) less well understood than in other countries (witness the casualness with which many commentators and policy makers have, in recent years, extolled the virtues of de-industrialisation and the shift to services, which, unfortunately, remain to be identified in so far as they are to generate enough employment to absorb the displaced industrial workers) (p.11).

In short, the conventional wisdom is that British manufacturing is 'in decline'. It might be reasonable to conclude therefore that, if Britain has an industrial culture, then it is a negative one.

But this has not always been so; the creation of the industrial and co-operative laboratories in the 1930s under the Department for Scientific and Industrial Research

(DSIR) and the outstanding performance during the Second World War was followed by intense government interest. For instance, the Barlow Committee on Scientific Manpower reported in 1946:

> Never before has the importance of science been more widely recognised or so many hopes of future progress and welfare founded upon the scientist[22].

Later, in 1964, the active support of technological advance in industry by Government was manifest in the creation of the Ministry of Technology. The expansion of university science departments and the creation of the technological universities was another manifestation of an emerging positive culture. Backed by the scientists and engineers in the government laboratories and the research associations, industry raised its own R&D expenditure to an all-time high in 1967. Qualified scientists and engineers in manufacturing rose from 94,000 in 1961 to 140,000 in 1971, an increase of almost 50 per cent[23].

In the years of the Ministry of Technology, close collaboration was achieved between government-sponsored laboratories and industrial companies, reinforced by a network of regional and university liaison officers. But this energy, enthusiasm and effectiveness in solving problems and achieving technology transfer – so admired and studied by other countries – faded with the 1970 dissolution of the Ministry of Technology. Scientists in the laboratories felt that they had lost their most important role. The new structure for the promotion and support of innovation, which was centred on the Requirements Boards[24], was more bureaucratic, less immediate and, by imposing charges for contract research and problem-solving at 'full economic cost', their services proved to be too expensive for many smaller companies – just where the need was greatest.

Despite the manifold problems arising from difficult labour relations, Stop Go and price controls, manufacturing output of the new technological industries more than compensated for the decline in output of textiles, ship-building and steel. Until 1974 the rise in output in British manufacturing almost equalled the average for all the developed market economies and was only 10 per cent less than in the United States.

An abrupt fall in output came with the oil price shock in 1973. The disabilities under which British manufacturing had been working, especially price control – which denied the premium for innovative products – had been weakening the technological base. Companies could not absorb a doubling of material prices at a time when the Price Commission was insisting on holding down selling prices. The number employed in R&D fell further. For instance in mechanical engineering, it fell by 50 per cent between 1969 and 1974. The number of insolvencies doubled.

The negative industrial culture explains why some economists could see no harm in price control – in place with variations from 1957 until the Competition Act of 1980 (see Appendix D), the idea being to prevent 'excessive profits'. Under price control companies were denied the margin that could have been earned had the new innovative product been priced according to the discipline of the markets or, at best, the increase was subject to up to six months delay. To the extent to which price control reduced takings, possibly as high as 7 per cent, this reduced disposable funds and so investment. In the United Kingdom investment takes half of available funds (Table 1, p.30).

The financial culture of the United Kingdom further complicates the situation. Because the value of shares is strongly influenced by current or expected dividends, companies may hesitate to extend their research programmes because the extra funds would have to be deducted from 'profits'. Thus the activities of the City add still another burden to a company trying to update its range of products. Sir Douglas Wass, Permanent Secretary to the Treasury until 1985, has similar reservations. In his Shell International Lecture 1988[25] he concluded:

> Finally, I think we have to stop thinking that industry is all about take-overs, mergers, dawn raids and so on. To read our financial press one would get the impression that those issues dominate management thinking. Again I contrast this situation with Japan and Germany. If management is continually having to think of a defensive strategy to avoid a predator; or if management can only think of expansion by take-over rather than by developing the existing business, we are likely to get pretty poor industrial performance. I have no specifics for stopping the take-over craze; nor would I want to interfere with the sort of industrial reorganisation which leads to greater efficiency. But I do not believe that it makes any sense for firms to come together for purely financial reasons when they have no common activity whatever.

United States

Because of its great size and freedom of movement, the United States has essentially a 'free-enterprise' culture, in which the Federal Government plays a very small part – the main area of support being in foreign trade. The vitality and mobility of manufacturing enterprises are shown by the fact that something like a third of capital assets are 'retired' each year; companies may be moving nearer to the market for the product or leaving behind recalcitrant labour.

Yet it must be remembered that companies in the United States have been influenced by the new 'business management' culture within which finance and organisation take precedence over product development. This approach has been unhelpful, for the accounting conventions taught to the post-war class of business managers pay little attention to research and technological change, seeing such disbursements as part of 'overheads'.

It is certain that in the 1970s the lack of funds set aside for intangible investment, the so-called 'manufacturing myopia', played a part in the loss of competitiveness after 1979. The Japanese attack on many United States markets from 1978 came as a severe shock and has affected confidence. There is some evidence that this has persuaded companies to spend even more of their cash on outside consultants, a procedure which has raised costs to unacceptable levels.

References to Part I

1. *R&D expenditure.* Data are available from the early 1960s from the following publications: *Industrial research and development expenditure and employment*, Business Monitor, MO14, Department of Trade and Industry, London (Annual); *Forschung und Entwicklung in der Wirtschaft*: Stifterverband für die Deutsche Wissenschaft, Essen (Biennial); *Research and development in industry*. Detailed statistical tables: National Science Foundation, Washington, USA (Annual); *Report on the survey of research and development.* Statistics Bureau, Prime Minister's Office, Japan (Annual). *Innovation.* See also, Charles Carter, Innovation and industry, *Policy Studies*, 7(4). 'The word 'innovation' comes from the Latin 'innovare', to renew or alter: it relates to the act of introducing a novelty, or of altering what is established by the introduction of new elements. It is not derived from invention, for that word comes from 'invenire', to come upon or discover'.
2. *Annual Report 1987*, Reckitt and Colman.
3. *Selected Statistics on Technological Innovation in Industry*, Statistics Canada, Catalogue 13-555, Ottawa, 1975.
4. *Statistisches Handbuch für den Maschinenbau*, Verband Deutscher Macshinen und Anlagenbau l.v., Fankfurt, 1988.
5. Lothar Scholz, *The IFO innovation survey – conception and results*. Paper presented at the 15th Atlantic Economic Conference, Paris, 1983.
6. *Innovation*, as defined by Statistics Canada, is as follows:
   Final product development and design engineering is the further modification of a product (process) after the research is completed in recognition of market or manufacturing requirements. For instance, it includes the costs of industrial design for aesthetic value, and for production drawing and specifications;
   New product marketing and market intelligence is the set of activities necessary for the successful introduction of a new or improved product (process) into the market. Its costs comprise those of market research, the non-recurring costs of establishing distribution and sales channels and advertising systems, as well as initial advertising expenditures;
   Tooling and industrial engineering covers all changes in production machinery and tools, in procedures, methods and standards to be used in manufacturing the new product or using the new process;
   Manufacturing start-up includes the costs of retraining personnel in the new techniques or in the use of new machinery, trial production runs and the costs of items damaged because of faulty equipment, procedures and operators' errors;
   Patent work is the filing of patent applications and searches for prior patents in connection with the product or process being introduced or improved.

7. Richard R. Nelson and Sidney G. Winter, 'In search of a useful theory of innovation', *Research Policy*, 6, 1977.
8. *Council Regulation (EEC) No 2176/84* of 23 July 1984. 'A product shall be considered to have been dumped if its export price to the community is less than the normal value of the like products'.
9. See *The Price and Pay Code*, February 1973. Cmnd 5247, for example, the instructions in paragraphs 34 to 36:
    Quantity or quality change, and new products
    34. A reduction in quantity or quality is equivalent for the purposes of the Code to a price increase.
    35. Quality change in goods or services, quantity change in sales units, or artificial creation of new products should not be used as a means of avoiding the requirements of the Code. Where the Price Commission form the opinion that this has been done, they may seek price reductions or disallow cost increases.
    Price reductions
    36. Where there is a fall in raw material prices or in other allowable costs, this should be fully reflected in price reductions. In addition prices should be reduced where other factors (such as an increase in the volume of sales since the last price increase) lead to a significant fall in allowable costs per unit.
10. It is of interest that D.A. Walker, Executive Director, Bank of England, speaking to the Glasgow Finance and Investment Seminar, 24 October 1985, stated that changes in the financial world, including the trend to institutional ownership of British industry, have contributed to short-term thinking.
11. Christopher Lorenz, *Investing in Success*, Anglo-German Foundation, London, 1979, p.11.
12. L. Iacocca, 'Competitive edge is costly to have', *The Japan Economic Journal,* 9 March 1987.
13. S. Gompertz, 'Pyramid buying by the tycoons of Tokyo', *Investors Chronicle*, 1 May 1987.
14. G. Golzen, 'Minding someone else's business', *The Times*, 14 May 1987. 'In the 1970s recession, management became sharply aware of the costs of high-priced inhouse expertise, if it is not fully used. If you are only deploying someone for 100 days you not only save the salary, you also save the fringe benefits.'
15. Shareholders' interest as percentage of total assets. See also Vittas, D. and Brown, R, *Bank lending and industrial investment*, Banking Information Service, 1982. Reported equity ratios in manufacturing:

	United Kingdom	West Germany	Japan
1976	39.4	27.4	17.0
1977	41.8	27.4	17.4
1978	43.5	27.1	18.4
1979	44.1	28.0	19.3
1980	45.7	27.2	20.6

16. J.M. Keynes, *General Theory of Employment, Interest and Money*, Macmillan, London, 1936, p.24.
17. Between 1972 and 1976 in England and Wales, the number of company liquidations doubled – from 3,063 to 5,939. *British Business*, 24 April 1981; *Economic Trends*, No. 257, March 1975.
18. R. Nelson, and S. Winter, 'In search of a useful theory of innovation', *Research Policy*, 6, 1977.
19. See C. Lorenz, *Investing in Success*, op.cit.
20. Keynes, J.M., *The General Theory of Employment, Interest and Money*, p.47.
21. Yao-Su Hu, *Industrial Banking and Special Credit Institutions: a Comparative Study*, Policy Studies Institute, London, 1984.
22 *Scientific Manpower*. Report of a committee appointed by the Lord President of the Council, HMSO, Cmd 6824, May 1946.
23. Census 1961 Great Britain, *Scientific and technological qualifications*, HMSO, 1962; also *Persons with qualifications in engineering, technology and science*, Census of population 1971, Great Britain, Department of Industry, 1976.
24. Department of Trade and Industry, HMSO.
25. D. Wass, 'What sort of industrial policy?', *Policy Studies*, 6(3), January 1988.

Tables and figures to Part I

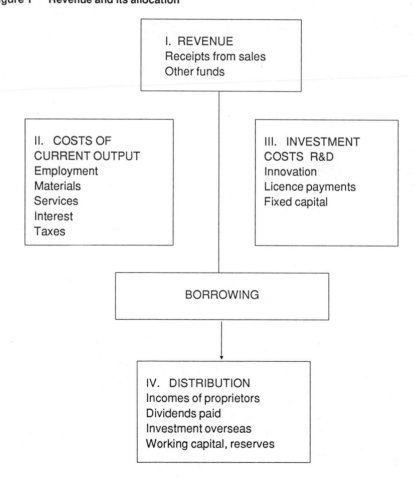

I. REVENUE
Receipts from sales
Other funds

II. COSTS OF
CURRENT OUTPUT
Employment
Materials
Services
Interest
Taxes

III. INVESTMENT
COSTS R&D
Innovation
Licence payments
Fixed capital

BORROWING

IV. DISTRIBUTION
Incomes of proprietors
Dividends paid
Investment overseas
Working capital, reserves

Table 1   Relationship between available funds and investment in mechanical enginering: as a percentage of the value of sales

	Available funds	For investment*	For distribution and working capital etc
United Kingdom			
1977	15.8	8.7 (0.9)	7.1
1982	16.8	9.5 (1.4)	7.3
1984	18.8	10.5 (1.7)	8.3
1985	18.3	9.6 (1.5)	8.7
West Germany			
1977	12.3	10.3 (2.5)	2.0
1982	15.6	12.0 (2.7)	3.6
1984	17.6	12.7 (2.9)	4.90
1985	19.2	12.6 (2.8)	6.5
United States			
1977	14.0	8.0 (1.2)	6.0
1982	16.7	9.9 (1.8)	6.8
1984	8.5	8.4 (1.8)	0.1
1985	8.7	8.6 (1.7)	0.1
Japan			
1977	7.8	6.8 (1.7)	1.0
1982	10.9	8.5 (1.8)	2.4
1984	8.5	8.0 (1.6)	0.5
1985	7.9	8.9 (1.6)	-1.0

* R&D percentages are in brackets

Table 2   Costs of employment and services for current output in the chemical industry: as a percentage of the value of sales

	Japan		United States	
	Employment costs	Services	Employment costs	Services
1980	7.2	13.8	11.8	16.2
1981	7.5	16.0	11.3	16.5
1982	7.5	17.4	12.5	19.5
1983	7.3	18.6	12.0	19.3
1984	6.9	19.2	11.3	19.6
1985	7.3	19.6	11.4	20.0

Source: Census of Manufacturing in United States and Japan; US Internal Revenue Service and Bank of Japan.

Figure 2   Central Bank discount rates

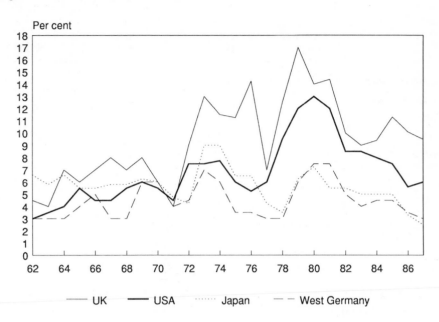

Table 3   Central Bank discount rates

Per cent per annum

	1980	1981	1982	1983	1984	1985	1986	1987
United Kingdom	14.0	14.4	10.0	9.0	9.4	11.3	10.1	9.5
West Germany	7.5	7.5	5.0	4.0	4.5	4.0	3.5	3.0
United States	13.0	12.0	8.5	8.5	8.0	7.5	5.6	6.0
Japan	7.3	5.5	5.5	5.0	5.0	5.0	3.3	2.5

Source: Bank of Japan, *Economic Statistics Monthly*

Table 4   Payments of interest for loans in 1985: as a percentage of the value of sales

	United Kingdom	West Germany	United States	Japan
Mechanical engineering	1.7	1.7	3.9	2.4
Motor vehicles	1.7	0.7	5.2	1.1
Electronics	1.3	1.5	3.2	1.4
Chemicals	2.0	1.0	3.0	2.5
Textiles	1.6	1.8	2.3	3.0

Table 5   Dividends paid: as a percentage of the value of sales

	United Kingdom	United States	Japan
Mechanical engineering	1.5	1.2	0.6
Motor vehicles	0.4	1.6	0.5
Electronics	1.8	1.1	0.6
Chemicals	2.6	3.2	0.6
Textiles	1.7	0.5	0.2

Table 6   Employment costs in mechanical engineering: as a percentage of the value of sales

	1972	1973	1974	1975	1977	1979	1982	1983	1984
United Kingdom	32	32	32	32	31	31	31	31	31
West Germany	31	31	32	36	36	34	33	33	31
United States	32	32	32	30	30	29	32	31	30

Source: Tables C1 to C3 (pp.135-137)

Figure 3   The dynamics of cash flow and employment for current and future output

CURRENT OUTPUT

FUNDS ALLOCATED	ACTION TAKEN	RESULTS OF ACTION
MATERIALS PURCHASED	TECHNOLOGICAL, COMMERCIAL AND LABOUR SKILLS ADD MARGIN TO PURCHASES	RECEIPTS FROM SALES
RECEIPTS FROM SALES	COMMERCIAL EXPERIENCE SHOWS PRUDENT LEVEL FOR EMPLOYMENT COSTS IF INVESTMENT IS TO BE MAINTAINED	EMPLOYMENT BUDGET
EMPLOYMENT BUDGET	EMPLOYMENT BUDGET DIVIDED BY UNIT LABOUR COST:	NUMBER EMPLOYED ON CURRENT OUTPUT

FUTURE OUTPUT

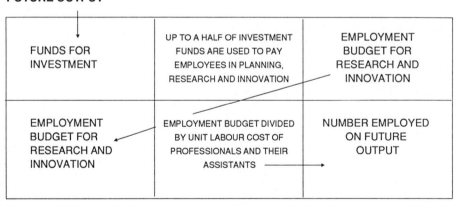

FUNDS FOR INVESTMENT	UP TO A HALF OF INVESTMENT FUNDS ARE USED TO PAY EMPLOYEES IN PLANNING, RESEARCH AND INNOVATION	EMPLOYMENT BUDGET FOR RESEARCH AND INNOVATION
EMPLOYMENT BUDGET FOR RESEARCH AND INNOVATION	EMPLOYMENT BUDGET DIVIDED BY UNIT LABOUR COST OF PROFESSIONALS AND THEIR ASSISTANTS	NUMBER EMPLOYED ON FUTURE OUTPUT

Table 7   Value added and investment in 1984

	Mechanical engineering	Motor vehicles	Electronics	Chemicals	Textiles
Value added as a percentage of sales					
West Germany	46	40	54	37	34
Japan	30	23	28	24	29
United Kingdom	47	34	52	36	36
United States	40	26	52	30	30
Investment as a percentage of value added					
West Germany	28	33	39	34	17
Japan	27	40	49	45	16
United Kingdom	22	38	44	32	14
United States	21	35	44	36	16

PART II

CURRENT COSTS AND INVESTMENT

IN FIVE INDUSTRIES

8   Concepts and presentation

As explained earlier, the conceptual approach to the assessment of the economic performance of manufacturing enterprises is straightforward. It starts from the annual sum of money which represents the revenue from the sale of the products (or money in) and continues with an analysis of the way in which this sum of money is disbursed to employees, suppliers, providers of loans, shareholders and tax authorities (money out).

The pattern of costs in a particular industry in any one year can be distorted by the vicissitudes of trade, and this makes inter-country comparisons difficult. What is needed to deal with this problem is a pattern of costs, the 'normal cost structure', which reflects the technological features of the industry but is timeless. The norms shown in the tables in Appendix C are based on empirical observations of the allocation of resources in each technology over the period 1972-1985.

It should be noted that the norm represents a balanced cost structure; in the financial jargon it is 'capital market based'. This means that finance for investment is largely self-generated but topped up with equity; so external debt and interest payments are low. Comparisons can therefore be made with cost structures that reflect a 'bank-based' policy, where current costs take a higher proportion of sales revenue and the banks provide the funds for part of investment expenditure.

Presentation

In contrast to the cash-flow models (as illustrated in Figure 1, p.29) which summarise the patterns of cash flow, the computer statements give these flows in detail. In addition, employment costs are shown in relation to the cost per head and numbers employed in each main category. The figures are presented first in national currency and then in relation to the value of sales and to value added. An example is given in Appendix B for mechanical engineering in West Germany in 1984. The figures relating to innovation are supplied by the German Machinery and Plant Manufacturers Association (VDMA) who undertook a detailed survey of costs in their industry in 1976, 1980 and 1984.

Five industries have been studied to show how the pattern of costs reflects both the technology that is being developed and the historical and legislative environment. Mechanical engineering represents an established industry producing mainly investment goods for industry and with minimum government involvement. Motor vehicles is a second traditional industry but one that has suffered severe difficulties, with retrenchment in some countries and expansion elsewhere. The electronics industry, by contrast, does extensive work for governments and is using and developing a rapidly advancing technology. The chemical industry provides its own internal contrasts, since it produces both high and low value added products and the mix is changing. Finally in textiles, we have another traditional industry that is adopting elements of high technology in both materials and processes.

In presenting the results a specialist vocabulary has been avoided. Certain abbreviations, in particular those referring to government policies, organisations, or special events – also the convenient acronyms – are described in the glossary (Appendix F).

9 Mechanical engineering

The mechanical engineering industry represents the largest group of companies constructing primarily investment goods, and this gives them a special relationship with their customers. Manufacturers increase their orders for new plant and equipment during a business upswing and hold off in the downswing, so the pattern of work is not even. However, the effect of such swings can be exaggerated; for instance from 1954 to 1974 the volume of output in the United Kingdom rose steadily and, apart from the recession in 1971/72, the 'troughs' were shallow.

United Kingdom
The output pattern for the mechanical engineering industry in the United Kingdom over the last twenty years is more or less comparable to the cyclical pattern followed by manufacturing industry as a whole, with a lag of one year. Manufacturers' own investment in fixed capital tends to respond to an upswing in output with a lag of about one year. For instance, while output in British manufacturing industry was at a peak in the boom year 1973, when gross domestic product increased by about 7 per cent, the peak for the mechanical engineering industries was reached in 1974. Within the sector there was a wide variation of experience: severe decline of the output in the textile machinery industry after the 1975 recession brought it down in 1983 to a level which is barely one-quarter of that in 1973; the output of the machine-tool industry has been declining also since 1974 whereas some other sub-sectors, such as fabricated constructional steelwork or boilers and process plant, recovered after 1979.

Between 1960 and 1970 output of mechanical engineering products rose by 50 per cent, keeping abreast of the United States and West Germany. Investment in 1967 was 11 per cent of sales – above the norm – with employment in R&D at its peak of 19,000 people. There are differing views regarding performance in the period 1963-70, the years when Britain had a Ministry of Technology. Did it represent the failure of the white hot technological revolution or was it a period of promise – a unique period of active and successful collaboration between industry, government officials and central laboratories? The statistical evidence for this industry is marshalled in Table 9 (p.65) It will be noted that, despite price control, the value added, overall investment and R&D (both expenditure and employment) were the highest ever recorded, while current costs at 85 per cent of sales value were the lowest.

With price control tightened by legislation, the rise in oil prices meant that current costs rose, reaching a peak in 1974. Accompanying the higher current costs (and certainly influenced by them) was a fall in R&D expenditure. The pattern of costs for this industry from 1968 to 1985 is shown in Table 8 (p.64).

The recession of 1971 and the rise in oil prices added to the difficulties of the industry. Material prices rose steeply after 1972 (Table 10, p.66). In 1974, the year of highest output, material costs rose to 51 per cent of sales received and the industry was in deficit, requiring substantial bank loans. Investment fell to 7.7 per cent of the value of sales in 1975 and employment in R&D declined correspondingly to half the level of 1967 (Table 9, p.65). The second oil price shock in 1979 raised the prices of raw materials a further 41 per cent – measured between 1978 and 1982.

The 1985 recovery in output followed a ten-year decline (Figure 4, p.67) yet in the years prior to 1974 the British industry had outpaced that of West Germany and continued to do so until 1977. Furthermore, nearly 50 per cent of the output of the British industry was exported throughout the period, so the loss of market share (11 per cent down to 8 per cent) reflected the lower output rather than the state of competitiveness. But why did output fall 25 per cent below the level of 1974?

First, it must be remembered that, during this period, the British economic scene was one of change and turbulence. Taking the most critical period 1970-74, these years saw the explosion of wage settlements under the Social Contract (September 1974), a state of emergency with power cuts, a three-day working week in February 1972, a further state of emergency with the fuel crisis in November 1972 and a second three-day working week in December 1973. Finally, there was price control.

Attempts to control producer prices, in the interest of counter-inflation, go back to August 1957 with the Council on Prices, Productivity and Incomes. But such control was not given statutory backing until August 1966, with fresh powers under the Prices and Incomes Act 1968. Prior to 1970 the TUC agreed a 3.3 per cent norm for wage increases, but actual increases were over 20 per cent and industry adjusted, but with lower margins and reduced employment (Table 9, p.65). So with the Pay Board and Prices Commission operating under the Counter Inflation Act 1973 (and the miners' strike of February 1974 causing further trouble) the situation changed.

It will have been observed that while prices of engineering products were held below those determined by the discipline of the market (a loss of anything up to 9 per cent of revenue) costs were rising steeply. The analyses of the cost structure show that, in 1962, costs for West Germany and Britain were similar but by 1974 the exogenous pressures on the British industry had seriously distorted the pattern of costs while those in Germany had changed very little (Tables C1, p.135 and C2, p.136). With sales revenue held down, the more expensive material inputs took 51 per cent – that is over half the sales revenue – compared with 41 per cent in 1968.

The industry in Britain faced material prices which in 1974 were 75 per cent above those of 1970, but was not permitted to raise its selling price beyond 54 per cent, and this after a delay of up to six months (Table 10, p.66). The result was an increase in material costs relative to sales revenue and so a drop in value added from 49 to 40 per cent of sales receipts. Substantial bank loans were required to meet the liabilities in 1974. By comparison the German industry had only slight problems; with encouragement from the Federal Government, selling prices rose faster than material prices; they were only slightly lower in 1974, and 1975 producer prices had again risen above those of material prices, and have remained so.

In the British industry matters were serious. Value added had dropped to 40 per cent of the value of sales in 1974 (compared with 52 in 1968) and with employment costs of 32 per cent to be met out of this, plus incomes of working proprietors and shareholders, expenditure on investment was squeezed and by 1975 had fallen to 7.7 per cent of sales value. Thus while in 1967 the British industry was spending more than the German on R&D, by 1975 it was spending only a third as much (Figure 4, p.67). The implementation of price control had meant that money, urgently required by the industry for product development to maintain competitiveness, had been left in the pockets of its customers.

Another feature of the cost structure in 1974 must be mentioned – namely the level of employment costs; these remained virtually unchanged at 32 per cent of sales revenue. This shows that employers can, and do, hold their employment costs down when other, uncontrollable, costs are increasing. It follows that when increases in wages are negotiated nationally, unless revenue rises by a corresponding amount, wage adjustment (to use the OECD expression) takes place and employees are made redundant, or posts vacated are left unfilled. In Table 9 (p.65), the index of output can be compared with employment between 1970 and 1974.

It can be argued therefore that price control which ran from 1968 until 1980 contributed to adverse effects in four areas:

• it unbalanced the cost structure of the British industry,

• by lowering the sales revenue it lowered the size of the employment budget, and so the number of employees,

• it reduced the level of investment overall, and the expenditure on R&D from 1.7 per cent of sales to 0.9 per cent

• it reduced the number of highly qualified manpower employed in investment activities from 19,000 to 10,000.

The comparison with investment in West Germany in Figure 5 (p.67) serves to emphasise the seriousness of this position. From 1973, West German expenditure on R&D never fell below 2.5 per cent of sales value, two or three times that of the UK industry which, from 1975, was drawn from a smaller sales revenue.

West Germany

Having noted the steady rise in output and the strong investment performance, it is somewhat surprising to find that costs of the mechanical engineering industry in West Germany were high over this period, the item mainly responsible being employment both for in-house staff and for those providing specialist services. This has not always been so; prior to 1975 the cost structure approximated to the norm. In the early years of the German 'economic miracle', wage demands were modest and contracts were of unusually long duration (one to two years) both in the 1966/67 down-swing and recession and the initial phase of the up-swing in 1968.

It is believed that the change, when it came, was an over-reaction. Furthermore, the rapid increase in profits, which accompanied the rising output, violated the principle of fair shares in income growth, the 'social symmetry' on which the Federal Government had promised to base its incomes policy. On their side, the employers were seriously concerned about the deterioration in industrial relations and wished to avoid strikes at any cost (see OECD *Economic Survey*, 1971). In consequence in 1970 they agreed wage increases of 12.5 per cent and the Government declared a commitment to maintain a high level of employment. This thinking gave the impetus for the establishment of Concerted Action through which wage rises were determined on a national basis. This development broke the link between changes in profitability and changes in wages – with the result that many companies had to agree to wage levels that were high relative to change in their sales revenue. As the cost structures in Table 11 (p.68) show, these changes resulted in a high cost industry; employment costs in 1975 rose to 36 per cent, four points above the norm, and outstanding debt was equivalent to 55 per cent of sales revenue, of which three quarters was short-term.

This situation brought a fall in profitability and a rise in interest payments. Nevertheless, expenditure on R&D fell only slightly and, to offset even this small fall, the Federal Government introduced a subsidy on payments to R&D personnel.

Table 11 (p.68) shows that employment costs remained high from 1975 to 1981 and decreased thereafter. By 1985 they had fallen below the norm. It is also possible that the higher wage levels encouraged the use of outside expertise including consultants, the cost of which was higher than the norm over most of the period.

The highest output was recorded in 1986 (Figure 4, p.67). Competition from Japan and other Asian countries became acute after 1978 and market share fell from 24 per cent to 20 per cent of total exports of OECD countries. However, by 1986 Germany had regained the highest market share with Japan coming second, and the United States third (Tables 52, p.119 and A1, p.124).

While it has to be admitted that causal relationships are very difficult to prove, in this instance the industries in Britain and West Germany started from a similar base and grew together until 1973. The trend of output diverged only after 1974 when the macro-economic policies of their respective countries took a different path. Even without giving due consideration to the effects of 'attitudes' and the movement of exchange rates, in the United Kingdom the explanation of the fall in competitiveness and loss of market share is in accord with common sense. Companies pursue research and innovation to maintain competitiveness and they fund these activities primarily out of their residual or 'disposable funds'. Thus if, for any reason, an industry is not allowed to charge the full market value of its products and disposable funds are attenuated, then its investment must be affected. Furthermore expenditure on capital assets has had considerable financial assistance from the British Government and it follows that, if funds for investment are restricted, the tendency in Britain is to cut research and innovation and to dismiss the technical manpower associated with it (Table 9, p.65).

The effect on output and on market share that accompanied the fall in R&D and innovation is clear from Figure 5 (p.67), and Table A1 (p.124).

United States

With $140 billion of sales in 1982, the United States mechanical engineering was five times that of Germany but only twice that of Japan. As might be expected in such a heterogeneous major industry the economic performance of the sub-sectors has been uneven. The industry as a whole has suffered from worldwide recession, the strong US dollar, high interest rates, and growing foreign competition in export and home markets. Thus the machine tool and textile equipment industries, for instance, have experienced since the 1970s a long period of depressed activity with lay-offs, plant closures, a shortened working week and losses due to widespread discounting of prices. In contrast, other sectors, e.g. oil-field machinery and components industries, had better performances and showed a strong recovery after the recession. The data provided by the US Department of Commerce, the US Department of the Treasury and the National Science Foundation used in this study, are aggregates of the six sectors of the industry.

The various sectors have been, and are, to a greater or lesser extent, going through a structural change based on a reduction of capacities where the product range was

41

uncompetitive. It is of interest that in 1982 costs of materials and employment, together accounting for 68 per cent of sales, are below the norm and suggest that structural adjustment has had a beneficial effect on factory costs (Table 12, p.69). But in contrast interest payments, taxes and expenditure on services are high in relation to sales. In particular, the increase in expenditure on miscellaneous services from 9 to 16 per cent between 1977 and 1985 is notable and partly offsets the lower costs elsewhere. It suggests that the improvements in technology and production control are not being paralleled by improvements in financial control. Put another way, from 1983 rapid product development and increased output have been made possible by increased research, joint ventures, offshore purchases and licensing arrangements (see also Table 21, p.74).

The overall costs for current output are computed mainly from three sources, the manufacturing censuses of 1977 and 1982, the annual surveys of manufactures, and the income returns of the US Internal Revenue Service. Table 12 (p.69) shows that current costs of manufacture took 98 per cent of the revenue from sales in 1984, substantially higher than the 'norm' or reference figure of 86 per cent. The detailed figures show that in 1982 the same proportion of sales revenue was allocated to employment costs (32 per cent), but 4 percentage points less was spent on materials. In contrast interest and tax payments were higher, both twice that of the norm.

Services, which took 16 per cent of sales revenue in 1982, rose to 19 per cent in 1984. This rise appears to be responsible for the increase in overall costs to 98 per cent despite a 2 per cent fall in employment costs for permanent employees.

The heavy reliance of the companies on outside services and expertise contributes to the relatively high costs in the mechanical engineering industries. Sub-contracting has remained at 3 per cent of sales value but there was an increase in the costs of miscellaneous services from 9 to 13 per cent between 1977 and 1982. This could reflect an increase in the costs of agents, consultants, factory removals, which, itself, may imply a general failure to control office expenses.

With regard to costs influenced by exogenous factors, including government policies, there are two which need to be stressed: interest payments and taxation. In 1977, interest payments represented 1.9 per cent of sales value or 4.1 per cent of value added. By 1982, interest payments took 8.4 per cent of the value added and 9.8 percent in 1984, despite the fall in interest rates (Figure 3, p.33 and Table 13, p.70).

In contrast, measures taken by the central government to lower the burden of taxation on industry have clearly reduced costs. Total tax payments fell between 1977 and 1982 from 6.4 per cent to 4.3 per cent of sales value, all of this reduction coming in the direct or 'income' taxes (Table 14, p.70).

To summarise, the analysis of current costs has shown that, while the pattern has changed over the five years, the total expenditure in 1984 represented 98 per cent of the value of sales, leaving 2 per cent available for all other purposes. This was too small to finance investment without funds from other sources (see also Table C3, p.132).

There has been a substantial increase in investment expenditure in relation to sales revenue. Between 1977 and 1982 it rose from 8.0 per cent of sales value to 9.9 per cent (see Table 15, p.70).

The figures support the belief that extensive restructuring was taking place from 1980. While purchases of fixed capital were high at 4.6 per cent of sales value, this must be interpreted in the context of retirements of nearly a third of this figure. This would suggest extensive closures followed by new start-ups, including those by foreign companies as a means of enlarging their market share. In addition, the increase in R&D expenditure and a 50 per cent increase in R&D manpower indicate a movement to higher value added and more competitive products in order to fight the increasing import penetration.

Japan

The output of the mechanical engineering industry in Japan is the second largest of the four countries studied. In recent years, there has been a further rise in the volume of output; a rise of 30 per cent occurred between 1983 and 1987. Generally the industry was expanding rapidly in the 1970s (in particular the machine tool sector in which numerically-controlled device-equipped equipment played a major role) in domestic and even more in export markets. In the early 1980s it suffered from world recession, sluggish domestic demand and curtailments of the national budget which, in particular, affected the construction machinery industry.

Under such circumstances, it is apparent that Japanese manufacturers engaged in price cutting competition, and accentuated the export effort to try to make up for decreased sales at home. Concomitantly, structural adjustment of the industry had been going on. Manufacturers were striving to cut production costs through streamlining and automation of production lines.

Analysis of the flow of funds shows that current costs are high in relation to the value of sales, being 9 percentage points above the norm in 1977 (Table 16, p.71). The rise in prices of imported raw materials after the oil price shock in 1974 provides part of the explanation of the imbalance; the other part being the inadequate demand and the price cutting that accompanied it.

The reasons for the imbalance in the cost structure become very apparent from the price indices shown in Table 17 (p.71). Though raw materials prices increased by 51 per cent between 1975 and 1985, they have since fallen below the level of 1975 (mainly because of the appreciation of the yen). The prices achieved for exports did not increase; and there was only a 10 per cent increase in the prices of goods for the home market.

In the situation before 1986 it was essential to raise additional funds, either as stock or as loans. Japan's savings rate is the second-highest of the OECD countries; over the last ten years the rate has averaged 20.2 per cent, second only to Italy with 21.7 per cent. West Germany has 12.7 per cent and the United States 6.5 per cent.

In the 1930s Japan's saving rate was only 5.8 per cent, and it is believed that the reasons for the large rise in savings in the post-war period reflects a higher level of income, but also the great insecurity about 'life after work'. The social security pension is low by European standards. Thus in general, Japanese savings should not be considered in the same light as savings in other countries, 'for Japanese do not withhold income which could be spent on having a good time, but rather they save because they are forced to, to survive after retirement'[1].

The assumption must be that these savings are more cheaply available to industry than in other countries – where parallel savings are held in pension funds – because Japanese savers are looking more for capital appreciation than for immediate income. If this is so, then it explains why industry feels freer to borrow and so under-pin the cash flow situation revealed in Table 16 (p.71).

The second notable feature is the low cost of in-house employment, only 18.5 per cent in 1985, including social charges. However, employment is supplemented by contract services costing 2,057 billion yen or 11.1 per cent of the value of sales. This suggests that an exceptionally high proportion of production work was done outside companies' own workshops and that the payments for the work of these contract employees could properly be added to employment costs. If contract services are included in employment costs, then the cost structure in 1982 becomes closer to the norm (Table 18, p.72).

Japan was badly affected by the first oil price shock; by 1976 the mechanical engineering industry had very high current costs and available funds of only 6.7 per cent. In consequence, investment was only 5.9 per cent, the lowest of the four countries (Table 21, p.74). However, it is notable that 54 per cent of this expenditure was allocated to research and innovation with an estimated 57,600 employees engaged in these activities. With this body of qualified people, product development and renewal of original models were greatly facilitated. The level of investment increased steadily and, by 1983, had reached an estimated 8.6 per cent of sales value, and 8.9 per cent in 1985. Expenditure on intangible investment remained higher than that on fixed assets – an important consideration in a world of increasingly competitive markets. Government tax relief and direct subsidies were also available to the industry in this period; they amounted to 1 per cent of sales value.

Expenditure on services remains high in the Japanese industry (Tables 18, p.72 and 19, p.72). The vertical integration of the production effort of large and small firms, using the contract services, is part of the answer but by no means all of it. It is probable that this higher allocation of resources to services originates both in the requirement of flexibility (and so the temporary employment of consultants and specialists) and in the changing requirements of foreign trade.

Interest rates have been exceptionally high in recent years and where an industry has suffered financial difficulties, it is to be expected that interest payments will rise. Beyond a certain point it becomes evident that the temporary assistance given by short- or long-term loans can exacerbate the costs crisis. As shown in Table 20 (p.73) the industry required additional cash after 1974 (following the first oil crisis) and, by the following year, interest payments had risen to 4.5 per cent of sales revenue. A fall in output of 20 per cent between 1974 and 1975 combined with the sudden rise in material costs had prompted additional borrowing. As short-term loans were repaid, the interest payments fell below 3 per cent.

Summary

There has been a massive change in the output and the market share of this industry in the four countries. Since 1960 Japanese output has increased nine times, almost doubling since 1970. From 1975 onwards the Japanese industry was challenging the United States, Germany and the United Kingdom particularly in machine tools. The fall in output was particularly steep in the United States over the 1981-82 recession.

In the United Kingdom, output fell steeply from 1974 to 1981. This was a period of great difficulty for British industry – higher material prices following the oil price shock, price controls and the 'winter of discontent' all added to the problems – but there is no way of saying how each negative factor contributed to the fall in output. Similarly, from 1979 the removal of price controls coincided with less labour unrest and, by 1982, balance had returned to the cost structure with R&D expenditure rising. These positive factors contributed to a substantial recovery in output – despite the strength of the Japanese competition and the renewed challenge from the United States.

10 Electronics

Electronics represents the new 'high-tech' manufacturing with considerable government involvement, in sharp contrast to mechanical engineering. Thus it is to be expected that overall investment will take a high proportion of sales receipts and, within this disbursement, intangible investment will take the lion's share.

By whatever measure is chosen, the electronics industry in the United Kingdom is small, about half the size of that in West Germany and one seventh that in Japan. The rate of growth of output over the five years 1980 to 1985 was much the same in the United Kingdom as in West Germany and the United States – averaging about 6 per cent per year – whereas in Japan the annual growth was 23 per cent per year.

Investment for the four countries is compared in Figures 8, p.76 and 9, p.76. The figure for Japan is lower than might be expected – though this is the direct result of a low value added (see Table C8, p.142).

United Kingdom

It would appear from the cost structures for the United Kingdom that value added of above 50 per cent of sales and high intangible investment are the hallmarks of a high technology industry (Table 22, p.77). Put another way, in view of the intense worldwide competition, there has to be a 'circle of survival'; that is, a high value added is required to finance the R&D for the rapid technological change, while high R&D is essential to achieve customer satisfaction, good prices and so the high value added. Thus to keep abreast of the world market, tremendous effort must go into both major and incremental change. The question to be answered is why the electronics industry in the United Kingdom has maintained the high value added in relation to sales and so a high level of research and innovation.

It is also of interest that since 1978 the overall level of investment was above the norm. Disbursements for fixed capital were tween 4.6 and 5.0 per cent of sales value (with one exceptional value in 1984); intangible investment, on the other hand, took 18-21 per cent – up to a fifth of all the money received from customers.

Defence contracts and their impact on the running of the electronics industry are much discussed in the literature. It is helpful therefore to examine the facts regarding the sales to, and those programmes of R&D and innovation undertaken for, the Procurement Executive of the Ministry of Defence.

Something like a fifth of the output of the electronics industry is undertaken for the Ministry of Defence, the proportion of sales being 17 per cent in 1980, 20 per cent in 1981 and 19 per cent in 1982. The programmes of R&D and product development undertaken to support defence procurement in electronics amounted to £284 million in 1982 or 19 per cent of defence R&D expenditure. This suggests that the 'research intensity' of work done in industry under MOD contracts is the same as that for civil programmes. This piece of evidence does not suggest that defence contracts are providing a subsidy for the investment carried out for the civil side of the industry: in fact there is some evidence to the contrary[2] It is of interest that, in 1981, MOD contracts represented about half of Government funding of R&D in electronics which, in its turn, was half of all R&D expenditure in industry.

The pattern of costs in electronics has reflected the typical British 'sound finance'. The industry has relatively low costs and thus is well able to finance investment out of the available funds of over 30 per cent of sales. The high intensity of R&D comes, therefore, as no surprise. The industry has selected its products in the high value-added range, so that it has low current costs but a high R&D intensity. In the process of picking winners it has clearly withdrawn from those items where the competition is fiercest, reducing employment for current output from 272,000 in 1980 to 224,000 in 1985.

West Germany

Measured in terms of both sales and employment for current output, the West German electronics industry is roughly twice the size of that in the United Kingdom (see also Figures 6, p.75 and 7, p.75).

Costs are however, considerably higher than in the United Kingdom; in 1984, they reached 86 per cent of the value of sales compared with 76 per cent in the UK. As in mechanical engineering, the main reasons for this are the high employment costs, 12 percentage points above the UK and 7 above the USA. In consequence, funds were insufficient for funding investment at 20-21 per cent, making the industry dependent on its 'other funds'.

United States

So many advances were made in the industry in the United States that the cost structure is of particular interest. The data show that throughout the period the material costs were equal to the norm, suggesting high technical efficiency, but the employment costs of company employees were 5 percentage points above. To this must be added the cost of external consultancy and other services were 6 percentage points above the norm in 1984. Reference to Table C7 (p.141) shows that the industry has considerable additional or 'other funds' equivalent to 8 per cent of sales revenue, and these funds are called upon to finance the investment of 21 per cent. Without these additional earnings investment would have been lower.

Japan

Even more surprising than the situation in the industry in the United States is that in Japan. This too proves to be a high cost industry – but the reasons appear to be quite different.

In recent years the Japanese industry has sold high quality goods at low prices, the primary aim being to expand its market share. Backed up with a high degree of market intelligence this commercial strategy has overwhelmed companies in Europe and the United States, so that market share has continued to grow. But the opportunity to raise prices above the introductory level, and so obtain an adequate sales revenue, has been obstructed by the emergence of industries in other countries of the Pacific Basin. Thus, in relation to a low revenue, material costs have been very high – 51 per cent in 1985. It will be noted also that employment costs of in-house employees in 1985 were only 11 per cent, but this low figure must be seen in conjunction with industrial services of 9 per cent and other services of 12.5 per cent (see Table C8, p.142).

The level of investment in relation to sales is the lowest of the four countries, 14 per cent or 6 per cent below the norm. However the estimated number of people in research and innovation, 190,000, is similar to the United States (see Figure 7, p.75). Technical knowledge is spread over a higher output.

How, with such an unbalanced cost structure, has the Japanese industry survived? One answer lies in the differing financial policies of Japanese companies compared with those of the United States or Europe. Japanese companies in high growth industries most often employ financial policies considered reckless and unmatchable by Western executives. According to Abegglen and Stalk[3]:

> The prevailing view is that Japanese companies can take financial risks because of the relationships they have with their financial institutions. Presumably their financial institutions reduce their risk by establishing close relationships with their clients through share holdings and access to better information.

The question is, can these procedures be viable in the long term? Already there are doubts. An article in *The Investors Chronicle* of May 1987 suggested that the Japanese themselves were getting worried because profits of industrial companies were falling significantly. It added that 'The root cause of all these problems is the soaring yen'. But, as the census data show, this is probably untrue. While the high yen will be an added problem for exporters in the short term, the true weakness lies in the imbalance in the cost structure; in practice the high yen helps to contain the biggest cost items, energy and material costs, and so should, on balance, be an advantage. An official of MITI noted, 'The high yen is a good thing and the direction is a good thing, but the speed of the yen's rise is causing some problems'. However, help was being provided to small and medium enterprises to give them time to adjust to the yen's rapid appreciation.

Summary

The cost structures found within this high technology industry are of particular interest. In a fast-moving technology expenditure on investment, both tangible and intangible, must be high – at least 20 per cent of sales value – and to achieve this, value added must be over 60 per cent. The industry in the United Kingdom has achieved this level of value added and West Germany came very close in 1983. Value added in Japan was only 28 per cent of sales value in 1984 and, in consequence, investment was low in relation to the value of sales (Table C8, p.142).

The results in Table 23 (p.78) raise a question regarding value added as a measure of economic efficiency. Have the recent changes in labour management made this measure out of date? As suggested earlier, growing expenditure on services is an alternative to paying for more employees and it can be argued, therefore, that services should be seen as an addition to labour costs in assessing productivity. It follows that the gross earnings (that is, sales receipts less materials and components) better reflect the totality of the companies' achievement; and this measure can then be studied in relation to labour costs, including extra-mural labour costs.

To summarise, the economic performance of the United Kingdom, with the smallest industry, has been the best in terms of achieving a balanced cost structure, and that of the second largest, Japan, has been the least good by Western criteria; it has very high material costs, a high expenditure on services and, in consequence, a low value added. The patterns of cost for 1984 are compared in Table 24 (p.78). It is of interest that expenditure on fixed capital is similar, above 5 per cent in all four countries; the difference lies in the resources devoted to research and innovation. The surprise result is that intangible investment in Japan is less than half that of the United Kingdom or West Germany when seen in relation to sales. The details of investment from 1972 to 1985 are given in Table 25 (p.79).

The low level of investment can be explained, at least in part, by a new development in Japanese industry. Professor Robert Reich at Harvard writes of the growing sophistication of Japanese attempts to gain technological know-how from abroad in view of the realisation that licensing agreements for new technology dispense with information only after the technology has been perfected rather than while it is under development. Japanese companies are becoming venture capitalists, taking shareholdings in small foreign technology-based companies, mainly in the United States[4]. Furthermore, the strength of the yen has decreased the purchase price of foreign shareholdings and the booming Tokyo stock market has made it relatively easy for Japanese companies to raise funds for overseas acquisitions.

While joint ventures are difficult to monitor in a country as far away as the United States, the Japanese persist because they take the view that the really innovative technologies come from that country. Professor Reich insists that in many cases Japanese companies have secured strategic stakes in United States business at bargain basement prices; 'they are extremely efficient in turning a technical breakthrough into a new process. They want to use the technology and bring it home.'

Thus while low level of disbursements on research and innovation in Table 25 (p.79) would seem to be inconsistent with what is known about Japanese success in this industry, joint ventures with companies in the United States, and possibly other countries, may be part of the answer. Even, more important is the collaborative research undertaken within the enterprise groups (or KEIRETSU) and supported by the powerful government laboratories. Seven such laboratories have been set up since 1981 and a new one, the Protein Engineering Institute, is scheduled to spend ten years on large-sale projects.

Import penetration is compared in Table A2 (p.125) for the four countries. To some extent import penetration is a cultural rather than an economic phenomenon, and becomes more a measure of the extent of 'goods exchange' than of economic performance. For example, in 1985 West German consumers paid $12.8 billion for electronics goods, of which $11.1 billion were imported – that is, 86.3 per cent. But the industry had sent $11.4 billion of its own electronics goods to other countries – so exports were $300 million larger than imports. Thus, in the true manner of the free market, while preference for certain foreign goods had increased imports, foreigners' preferences for German goods had increased exports to an even greater extent! Japan, on the other hand, preferred Japanese goods to the extent of 94 per cent of consumption and exports were only 28 per cent of their sales.

The strength of the Japanese electronics industry is also demonstrated by market share which was 33 per cent of OECD exports in 1985, compared with 19 per cent in 1970. The main loser appears to be West Germany, though, as in mechanical engineering, the exchange principle is operating. Exports are slightly higher than imports, production has remained above consumption for the whole period.

11 Motor vehicles

The third engineering industry, motor vehicles, combines the traditions and techniques of a traditional industry with rapid incorporation of the newest technologies. Of the four industries to be discussed, the interest lies in comparing the three European industries with a considerable history of development going back to before the First World War, with that of Japan which entered the field after the Second World War. It is a story of the greatest take-over bid in history, and the manner in which those most affected made their response.

United Kingdom

In his book, *Motor Cars: A Maturing Industry*, Daniel Jones points out that, until a decade or so ago, the motor car industries could be regarded as playing a locomotive role in Western European economies, their output increasing faster than total GDP[5]. This role has proved unfortunate for the British industry because it encouraged the Government to regulate it in the interests of macro-economic policies, the so-called 'Stop Go' policies. However, despite these interruptions, British output climbed until 1973, but the cost structure became unbalanced (Table 26, p.80). Under price control, the industry was not receiving the market price for its product, while union pressures were raising employment costs – from 21 per cent of sales to 33 per cent. With the lower margin that the vehicle companies were permitted to earn, the lower was the research, design and production engineering that they could fund. Furthermore, the less competitive the industry became through lack of product development and market intelligence, the more the Government was inclined to intervene. For example, the Labour Government entering office in 1964 began to pursue an active policy of direct intervention in the industry, among other things establishing the Industrial Reorganisation Corporation (IRC) to promote restructuring.

As shown by the index numbers of output in Figure 10 (81) and as described by Daniel Jones, the British Motor Corporation (BMC) formed in 1952 had expanded within the buoyant markets of the 1950s and 1960s; in the early 1960s it concentrated on the Mini and 1100 which were technically successful but, due to price control, never profitable. However, Daniel Jones concluded that 'The major weakness lay both in management, especially in production and design management and in industrial relations'.

Analysis of the cost structure for the period shows why design management was inadequate. As noted by observers at the time, if the prices of a popular product are limited to conform with counter-inflationary policies, then money is retained by the purchasers which should have been spent on research and other intangible investment to ensure the next generation of vehicles. In contrast, the German industry, pursuing a vigorous programme of R&D and product development (Figures 11, p.81 and 12, p.82), was able to add 12 units of value to every 10 spent on materials; whereas in Britain only 6 were added, a difference of 100 per cent at a time (1968) when the application of technology to industrial processes was given high priority by the British Government.

This is an acute case of the left hand not knowing what the right hand was doing. Yet expenditure on new plant and machinery was relatively high (Figure 13, p.82), a feature also characteristic of Britain – the idea that spending on new equipment is more important and less risky than that spent on research and innovation.

The second characteristic of a nationalised industry is the inability to control labour costs. Table 26 (p.80) shows how the pattern of costs became distorted in the 1970s by the explosion of wage settlements – employment costs rising from 21 per cent of sales to 33 percent in 1980. Despite job losses of 200,000, current costs rose above the value of sales in 1980. As shown in Table 27 (p.83) massive Exchequer support, £520 million – equivalent to 19 per cent of employment costs – was required to finance British Leyland in 1981.

In any future government policies to counter inflationary tendencies, it is to be hoped that more consideration will be given to the long-term future of the companies which can so easily be damaged irreparably by short-term actions of Government.

Table 28 (p.84) has arranged the same information under some simple historical headings. The figures must be read in the context of the fall in output documented in Figure 10 (p.81).

West Germany

Table 29 (p.85) shows the pattern of costs in the motor vehicle industry in West Germany. It has one thing in common with the United Kingdom industry – they have both been unable to control employment costs. So, although costs of current output were lower in Germany than in the UK, the available funds were too small to finance the required programmes of investment, and German companies were forced into a permanent borrower situation. Interest payments are low – reflecting the lowest interest rates of the four countries.

In 1967, a year of high investment in research and innovation as well as in fixed assets (7 per cent of sales) in the UK, the difference between Britain and Germany was small. But from 1967 to 1971 the gap grew to 7 percentage points and by 1972 German investment in R&D was twice that of Britain. Yet from 1971 to 1976, even in West Germany, the investment percentage fell steeply (Table 30, p.85). It can be shown that the causal factor of falling investment was primarily an imbalance in the cost structure which brought down disposable funds from 10 to 6 per cent in 1980. This drop reflected a diversion of funds to employment costs; together the costs of materials and employment had risen 10 points above the norm of 72 per cent of sales.

With disposable funds at only 7 per cent in 1977, roughly half what would have been expected, expenditure on investment had to be cut. Again, 60 per cent of investment expenditure is devoted to research and innovation, so these activities took the major share of the economies. Thus the levelling-off of R&D between 1971 and 1973, noted at that time by OECD, actually a fall involving the loss of a quarter of R&D employees, can be explained in terms of cash re-allocation (Figure 11, p.81). The employment budget in 1977 was 7 per cent above the empirical norm and it was increasingly difficult to shed labour. In contrast, the quality of the product is indicated by the high gross earnings – that is, the sales revenue less materials purchased for production.

The West German industry has maintained a high rate of investment in fixed capital from 1980 to 1982 – equalling that spent on the intangible assets of research and innovation. Figure 12 (p.82), showing the changes in the volume of output, compared with that of the United Kingdom, would suggest that the high level of overall investment since 1980 has provided a firm base from which to meet the competition of Japan and USA.

United States

The Americans also have a high-cost industry, and the cost items most responsible were materials and interest payments. In 1981 costs of current output exceeded the receipts from sales, leaving nothing for investment or for distribution.

The high cost of manufacture was partially offset by the 'other funds', in particular income from previous investments abroad (either parent companies or subsidiaries) and sales of discarded plant and machinery. Nevertheless, there was an overall deficit from 1980 to 1982.

Looking at the pattern of costs (Table 31, p.86), it is clear that material costs are even higher than in Japan though the United States industry can buy its materials on the home market. Such a low gross margin confirms that the United States companies were not keeping up with the competition from Japanese and European firms, and sale prices were lower than they would have wished. The other matter of interest is the very low and falling employment costs.

In this connection the disbursements on fixed assets are of particular interest (Table 32, p.87). They were low from 1972 to 1979 but rose steeply in 1980 and 1981 – suggesting a complete capital restructuring with some plans brought forward to meet the crisis. The disbursements on research and innovation remained above those of the other countries for much of the period (Table 35, p.90). Total investment was above that of West Germany in 1980, with R&D expenditure at the highest level recorded in United States or in the other countries.

Japan

The motor vehicle industry in Japan has grown very rapidly; output quadrupled between 1971 and 1980. Yet, as will be seen from Table 33 (p.88) it has become a high cost industry, though one that has a totally different cost structure from those of the United Kingdom and West Germany. The costs of materials, components and fuel are between 62 and 66 per cent of the value of sales. This would be untenable if it were not offset by employment costs of 10 per cent – only half the norm of 22 per cent. When services are included, the difference is equally dramatic – nearly 10 per cent below this cost item in Europe.

Investment was only a little below the norm. The amount spent on intangible assets was higher than that on fixed assets in all years – a further proof that research and innovation takes priority in Japan. Investment was financed from the sales revenue plus other funds in all years, but the surplus for distribution was very small, scarcely enough to pay the dividends.

Material costs are high in Japan because they have to be imported. But in addition, because the Japanese industry tends to keep its prices low, its revenue is correspondingly depressed; in terms of the cost structure arithmetic, this increases the relative cost of materials and decreases the gross margin and the value added.

As is well known, the strategy of discounted prices is highly effective in increasing growth and market share; but clearly it leaves the industry in a vulnerable position, one requiring massive support from shareholders and other savers. It has been suggested that

European companies could not survive with such 'aggressive' financial policies, whereby growth is financed from heavy borrowing at low rates of interest, and with dividend payments of under 0.5 per cent of sales receipts (compared with 1.6 per cent in the United States).

This example of Japanese industrial policy illustrates the problems of comparing economic performance. In the chosen industrial sectors Japan combines excellence in marketing and technological skills, providing a quality product of great commercial relevance. But, to ensure growth in market share, it sells at discounted prices and offsets the loss of retained income by borrowing at a low rate of interest from Japanese savers and institutions, thus putting itself in a permanent borrower situation. These aggressive financial policies have disadvantages; the industry is vulnerable not only to downturns in world trade, but also to new competitors in Asia. Furthermore, companies in the United States accuse the Japanese of dumping and study the case for protection.

So do aggressive policies of this type represent good performance? Or are they a short-term expedient justified only when a country wishes to break into a new market? The rise in output is undeniable, but the German industry has achieved much the same performance using more traditional financial methods while maintaining high quality.

In assessing good performance, it is also relevant to look at employee incomes – in 1985 Japan allocated about 10 per cent of sales revenue to its own employees, whereas in the German industry, employees received 30 per cent. Expenditure on services from outside the company were the same in the two countries – at about 12 per cent of the value of sales.

Summary

A study of the situation in the four countries is valuable because it serves to illustrate both the different relationships that can exist between industry and Government and the speed at which a once over-confident industry can respond positively to growing competition. Output trends for the four countries are shown in Figure 10 (p.81), R&D expenditure in Figure 11 (p.81) and fixed capital in Figure 14 (p.91).

The German industry has had, without any doubt, the best general environment. Despite the crisis in 1974 it has had good industrial relations, with both Federal and Länder Governments standing back until they gave support at a critical time. In contrast, the British motor vehicle industry has had to suffer the most adverse circumstances. In the 1970s, it became an instrument of government policies for counter-inflation and rationalisation mergers. The industry in the United States initially suffered from Japanese imports but it raised investment and renewed its challenge in 1985. The Japanese industry went for quality and high market share, literally at any price.

While the German industry continued to grow in a steady commercial environment with good industrial relations, the British industry was subject to a variety of government interventions – that included 'Stop Go' policies, mergers, price control – alongside restrictive practices, damaging strikes and imposed wage settlements that bore no relationship to performance. With such preoccupations, and with the reduced revenue resulting from price control, investment in R&D fell steeply and research and design teams were cut (Figure 11, p.81). In consequence the industry had little technological or marketing strength to face the Japanese and German competition. Output fell between 1973 and 1982 and market share declined further (Figure 15, p.91). With the ending of price control in 1980, investment recovered, and the upturn in output in 1987 suggests a return to competitiveness – though with the industry much smaller than hitherto.

In Germany the high quality product appears to have suffered little from Japanese competition and, if companies continue to lower their costs of materials, (and also their expenditure on services) it should be possible to maintain the high level of investment without further borrowing.

The industry in the United States suffered directly from Japanese competition and with the recession output fell dramatically between 1978 and 1980. However, the response to Japanese competition was a steep rise in investment from 1980 to 1982. A recovery of output followed – suggesting that lessons had been learnt. The suggestion that, in the late 1970s, the American industry had become complacent, is strengthened by the raised investment levels after 1980 followed by the rise in output (Table 35, p.90). It appears that American cars have renewed their challenge.

Finally, Japan. This industry has used, very effectively, all the strengths made available to it by its outstanding use of new technology and market intelligence. However, materials and components have remained a high cost item, partly because they must be imported, but also because cars have been sold (in both domestic and overseas markets) at low prices (their indices suggest that domestic prices, Yen basis, have not been raised since 1980). Had the balance of material and output prices followed that of, say, Germany, then one might have expected prices to have been 20 per cent higher. Undoubtedly this degree of price discounting made them price competitive with an increased market share: but at a high cost to the financial viability of the industry. Investment has been below the norm since 1979, reflecting the lower disposable funds and so a level of R&D below that of the United States and West Germany.

Much of the story of the motor vehicle industry is told in Table A1 (p.124) and Figure 15 (p.91) which show changes in market share since 1970. The Japanese share has risen from 9 per cent in 1970 to 29 per cent in 1986 – the displacement being from the United Kingdom (10 per cent down to 3.3 per cent) and from the United States (18 per cent down to 13 per cent).

What does this imply for the future? The UK industry has re-structured and has raised its level of R&D with the growing emphasis on quality. With the smaller volume of output and some investment from overseas it can be expected to hold its own in international markets. In the United States the recovery in output (Figure 10, p.81) is mirrored in a 4 per cent increase in R&D expenditure (in constant dollars) and substantial new equipment. In 1982 market share in Germany at 23 per cent was higher than in 1970 and very little lower than that of Japan. It has fallen in recent years but, by 1986, had recovered, reflecting output that was 50 per cent above the 1970 level and an all-time record (Figures 10, p.81 and 15, p.91).

12 Chemicals

The chemical industry has one of the highest concentrations of employees qualified in science and engineering and is among the highest spenders on research and development. The fact that such expenditure can be over two-thirds of that on fixed assets confirms its credentials as a science-based industry. However, while all were science-based, the pattern of costs in the four countries was markedly different. The West German industry in 1984 spent 8 per cent more of its receipts on employment and 8 per cent less on materials than in the United Kingdom (Table 43, p.99).

In view of the similarity of patterns of money-flows to those found in engineering, this divergence raises some interesting and important questions. These include:

*   Does the explanation lie in the proportion of final products sold? In other words, did the industry in the United Kingdom concentrate on lower priced general chemicals and the other on higher priced pharmaceuticals, dyestuffs etc?
*   Is it possible that production in the West German industry was less automated? That is to say, did West Germany spend a smaller proportion of sales receipts on plant and machinery and more on investment in research and innovation?

It has been found that there is little difference in the mix of products, if anything the British industry gains a higher proportion of its sales receipts from final products than does the West German industry. Furthermore the structure is similar; there is a similar degree of integration. This suggests, therefore, that the answer lies in the quality of the chemicals and so in the price obtained, rather than in the mix of products sold. What is clear is that the German pattern of sales enables a much higher proportion of sales receipts to be paid to employees; in 1985 this was 21 per cent compared with 13 per cent in the United Kingdom (Table 43, p.99). If this is the result of the industry moving progressively towards sales of higher quality, higher priced products, this could be an important finding.

If the hypothesis regarding the emphasis on quality rather than volume is correct (and there is anecdotal evidence that it is) then one would expect that the production processes with the lower employment costs would depend more on large automated plants and less on research and technological innovation. This hypothesis can be checked by reference to two standard indicators, investment in R&D and in fixed assets. The data show that from 1982 the German industry has spent more on research and development than it has on fixed assets while, in the British industry, the reverse is true (Table 42, p.98).

United Kingdom

Technological change in the chemical industry in the United Kingdom had a slower start than in West Germany or the United States. Research and development was on a small scale before the 1950s, technical expertise being employed largely for the testing of standard products to maintain quality.

Research grew rapidly after the Second World War, but was orientated more towards large integrated plants than to speciality products with a high value added.

In the 1970s accountants advised that speciality chemicals with a low volume of sales were 'too expensive' to produce, and the manufacture of many items was discontinued. The rise in material prices after the oil price shock made this a worrying trend, for the high material costs were associated with low value-added products. Employment costs fell as production of the high-volume general chemicals became more automated, from 17 per cent in 1972 to 13 per cent of sales value in 1985.

Total investment was 13.2 per cent in 1985, (Table 36, p.92) approaching the norm of 14 per cent with intangible investment at 7.5 per cent – the highest level recorded (Figure 16, p.100). The lack of emphasis on research and innovation in earlier years may explain why the British industry had a rate of growth which was well below that of the other three countries (Figure 17). Pharmaceuticals are of growing importance.

R&D expenditure has been rising since 1975, but in 1985 was well below that of West Germany (Table 42, p.98 and Figure 18, p.101).

The oil price shock raised the price of material inputs and Table 36 measures the impact on costs in this industry. By 1977, the proportion of sales that had to be allocated to materials had risen by 10 per cent in Japan (the most vulnerable country (Table 40). The UK and the USA were similar, with a rise above the norm of over 8 per cent. In both countries there is evidence that employment costs were reduced in an endeavour to compensate for higher material prices; and this change was accompanied by a sharp rise in expenditure on fixed capital (see Figure 19, p.101 and Table 42, p.98).

West Germany

The output of chemicals in West Germany has risen more slowly than in the USA and Japan but faster than in the United Kingdom (Figure 17, p.100). It remains a high cost industry, with disposable funds only about half the level of the early 1970s and reliance on 'other funds' for investment. However, although overall investment has fallen – reflecting the fall in disposable funds – the concentration on quality has remained. Research and development reached 5.1 per cent of sales in 1985, easily the highest of the four countries. To permit this there has been less emphasis on fixed capital (see also Tables 42, p.98 and C14, p.148).

The German industry has, therefore, put the provision of speciality chemicals of high quality and reliability above pressures for greater quantity of sales, based on a higher degree of automation – until recently almost the reverse of the situation in the United Kingdom.

The chemical industry in West Germany has been transformed into a high cost industry because of the expenditure on outside services, which have been 15 per cent since 1980. This is 50 per cent above expenditure in the 1960s and would imply a tendency to increase the contract work on maintenance of plant and the subcontracting of some steps in the chemical process to specialists.

United States

Output in the United States has shown consistent growth since the early 1960s, the only break in the trend coming in 1982. It has consistently outpaced Japan (with half the output of the United States) and has grown faster than West Germany.

Unlike West Germany and Japan this has been a low cost industry; only from 1980 did costs rise significantly above the norm. Employment costs of in-house staff fell between 1972 and 1981, presumably to be replaced by outside services. This would seem to be a fully co-ordinated operation in which greater flexibility was achieved. But, from 1981, there is some evidence that this policy of using outside expertise is increasing without a corresponding reduction in employment costs.

The high level of output has been maintained with the help of a rising number of employees working in research and innovation, estimated at 145,000 in 1983 of which 95,000 were in R&D (Figure 20, p.102). R&D as a percentage of sales was lower than in the UK and Japan until 1981, but has since been rising steeply. In actual manpower the industry has a dominant position as becomes its size; but it is of interest that it has widened the gap between itself and the industry in Japan.

This is a balanced and successful industry which is showing all the signs of maintaining its position by increasing investment and manpower and raising its R&D intensity. It is notable that the cost of outside expertise was very high from 1982, but the industry was offsetting this cost by reducing expenditure on in-house employees – down to 11 per cent in 1984. The fall in the proportion could be associated with the very high cost per head of employees in the chemical industry (twice that of the British industry, and over 50 per cent higher than in West Germany and Japan). The vigour of the industry is also demonstrated by the direct investment abroad by US companies. The amount invested has quadrupled since 1982 and the income from overseas investments has tripled.

Japan

Japan has the third largest chemical industry (measured by the value of its sales); it is roughly half the size of the industry in the United States, but three times that of the United Kingdom.

In terms of growth measured by the index of output, Japan comes second to the United States; in 1986 output was 90 per cent higher than in 1970.

The high rate of growth was, however, accomplished in the face of cost restraints. Prices of raw materials rose steeply after the oil price shock, raising material costs (relative to sales revenue) by 10 per cent and total current costs by 5 per cent, with no improvement recorded up to 1982. Employment costs were extremely low, just over 7 per cent after 1980, but outside services took twice that amount.

Outstanding loans and discounts reported to the Bank of Japan were equivalent to 40 per cent of sales revenue. Interest payments have been considerable: between 3 and 4 per cent but, since 1973, dividend payments have been below one per cent.

Between 1980 and 1987 export prices fell by 21 per cent and domestic prices by 18 per cent (Table 41, p.97). Despite this fall, production capacity rose by 7 per cent and the operating rate by 8 per cent.

In Japan chemicals remains a high cost industry, with total investment and R&D and innovation falling below the norm after 1972. However, intangible investment was higher than that on fixed capital which, at 3.9 per cent in 1985, was low for a process industry. Expenditure on services is very high but, unlike the industry in West Germany, the use of outside expertise is associated with very low, and falling, employment costs. This procedure reduces the companies' responsibility for the individuals in life-time employment, and so is understandable as an alternative policy for employment – giving maximum flexibility and permitting companies to adjust quickly to changes in world markets and advances in technology. Contract payments may also contain payment for new control equipment etc.

The two sets of production indices in Table 41 (p.97) help to explain the 90 per cent rise in output (Figure 17, p.100), where increased capacity associated with lower prices enabled the Japanese industry to challenge that of the United States. Nevertheless, the falling prices and high costs of materials and services resulted in a value added of only 25 per cent of sales value in 1985, two thirds of that in the industries of the United Kingdom or Germany.

The cost structures of the chemical industry in Japan describe an economic performance unlikely to be seen in Western countries: they represent a situation in which the growth of market share takes precedence over disposable funds. Japanese savers accept that their money is being used in the national interest and for capital appreciation rather than to produce dividends. The figures are consistent with the statement that Japanese industrialists have little interest in profits, only in market share.

Nevertheless, people concerned with the industry were growing anxious about the situation. Shuji Yamamoto of the Industrial Bank of Japan wrote as follows in 1986[6]:

> More effort is thus necessary than just preventing a price collapse by maintaining orderly market conditions. There must be a commitment on the part of individual companies to advance into greater-value-added products and to diversify their lines of business.

Summary
The chemical industry is distinguished by steady growth in the four countries with Japan and the USA doubling their output since 1970. The international exchange of chemicals – both crude and speciality – makes figures of import penetration hard to interpret. For instance, one country with the highest market share also has the highest import penetration. The British industry, with the second largest market share, has the second largest import penetration (Tables A1, p.124 and A2, p.125). Manpower engaged on research in the United Kingdom in 1985 remained well below that of Germany, 31,000 compared with nearly 54,000 (Figure 20, p.102).

13 Textiles

Textiles is a traditional industry. In the United Kingdom in the early years of this century it was the largest manufacturing employer. Despite the rise of the engineering and chemical industries, textile output continued to rise in all four countries up to the early 1970s. The emergence of the Asian producer soon after the Second World War affected growth but did not eliminate it. It needed the oil price shock in 1973 to change the trend. The effect was so sharp that arguments were heard that the textile industry in the West should be abandoned and left as the prime income earner of Asian countries. In the event some output was lost in Europe and Japan, but in the companies that remained greater emphasis was given to high value added goods.

United Kingdom

With textiles we are examining an industry which dominated employment in the first Industrial Revolution. When the first census was taken in 1907, the industry was already a century and a half old. It had a work force of 1,250,000 and sales that made up a quarter of all manufacturing sales, but by 1980 sales were only 3 per cent (Table 44, p.103).

It is clear from the earlier census data that the margin added to the materials purchased needed to cover fewer costs than today – for entrepreneurs would design and make their own modifications, while machinery and factory maintenance could be handled by local craftsmen. Thus from 1907 to 1924 the margin added to materials purchased was around 30 per cent, a mark-up so low that it could barely cover today's employment costs.

But from the early 1920s there were important changes. Research laboratories were established in the larger companies and co-operative research was undertaken under the sponsorship of the Department of Scientific and Industrial Research (DSIR). The efficacy of the resulting innovations in fibres and new designs became evident from the census results; the margin added to materials rose steadily, first to 37 per cent in 1930 and then to 40 per cent in 1935. In the 1950s the industry had, by modernising its approach to marketing, innovation and new designs, gone more than half the way from its traditional modes and practices to a cost structure which was viable in the technological age.

Furthermore the immediate post-war years saw an enormous pent-up world demand for textiles – but also the emergence of new producers of cheap textiles in Asia. So this strong demand should have provided the British industry with the opportunity to complete the conversion from mass-produced to quality 'up-market' goods, and to raise the gross earnings to the 52 per cent needed for a balanced cost structure. However, under the exigencies of the Government 'Recovery Programme', this was not to be. An American commentator at the time wrote of the problems met by the British industry. Under the 'utility' cloth programme the industry worked to detailed specifications for standardized products and, while such control gave experience in the mass production of certain cloths, the report concluded that these were 'not the type of product in demand by their foreign customers'[7].

Thus the Government and its advisers failed to appreciate that, had the industry been permitted to earn the higher receipts from quality products sold to a hungry world market, it could have funded adequate investment and completed its progress to complete viability. Until 1951, companies were geared to mass-produced products that remained in competition with Asian producers; and in later years the low margin permitted under price control ensured that investment in innovation and artistic design was further restricted. The sorry story epitomizes the hazards of government interference which, in the interest of a short-term programme of fair shares, jeopardised the longer-term programmes of research and product development.

So the opportunity to build on the advances made in the pre-war decade and to complete the steps to commercial viability was lost. Even worse, the trend became retrogressive and, by 1951, the margin added had fallen to 28 per cent – an abysmally low level never before recorded. It took another seven years for the industry to recover the trading position reached in 1935. It is ironic that the British Government, while impeding further innovation by its controls, appointed a Cotton Industry Working Party in 1946[8],

> to report as to the steps which should be adopted in the national interest to strengthen the industry and to render it more capable of meeting competition in the home and foreign markets.

Despite these problems, the output of textiles as measured by the index increased until 1973. The margin added to material purchases remained at much the same level, and, although costs of current output were high, the available funds were large enough to fund investment of between 4 and 5 per cent of sales value (Table 46, p.104).

In 1952, the controls on output to utility specifications were dropped in the 'bonfire of controls', and by 1968 the margin added to materials had risen from 30 to 44 per cent of sales – a substantial improvement but still below that of Germany. However, one control was substituted for another; the utility cloth programme went but price control took its place and no further improvement in margins was recorded until 1980. However, the cumulative weakness in research and innovation became apparent with the oil price shock. By 1977 price control had held the rise in prices of home sales 50 per cent below the rise in prices of the materials that companies had to purchase. The two negative effects triggered a massive fall in output (Figure 21, p.105 and Table 45, p.103).

West Germany

As will be seen from the pattern of costs (Table 47, p.105), the West German industry has concentrated on high value added textile materials and products; the margin added to purchased materials has rarely dropped below 50 per cent. This probably explains why the market share overtook that of Japan in 1973 and, in 1985, was 3 per cent higher. Disbursements for employment for current output were 5 per cent above the norm up to 1982, though they fell in 1985. Expenditure on services was also high, 2 percentage points above the norm in 1985, and the outcome was a high-cost manufacturing process.

As will be seen in Table 51 (p.109) investment was considerably higher than in the other three countries. Although this level of expenditure was achieved with the aid of new borrowing, the rise in market share suggests that it was a worthwhile investment.

United States

The industry in the United States has a lower margin added to materials than in West Germany – in recent years it has been only 42 per cent – but it compensated financially by employment costs that are 2 to 3 percentage points below the norm. Services were rather below the expected level. Output has fluctuated but has grown faster than in Japan.

Investment was funded with the help of 'other funds', including foreign investment and the surplus was, in most years, adequate to provide a small income for entrepreneurs and shareholders (Table 48, p.106).

Japan

The cost structure in the Japanese industry suggests that, in all the years studied, it was meeting intense competition worldwide; output fell by 16 per cent between 1973 and 1986. The price indices in Table 49 (p.107) suggest that sales receipts were lagging behind manufacturing costs. Prices for textiles sold in Japan fell 4.6 per cent between 1980 and 1986 and, as a further measure of the intense competition, the index of output prices, based on 1975, has risen more slowly than input prices.

Substantial loans were required in most years – an element of 'aggressive' financial policies to maintain market share. This financial strategy was associated with high employment costs. Full-time employees were allocated only 19 per cent of sales receipts in 1984 (below the norm), but additional work done by outsiders cost a further 18 per cent. Although Japanese output fell by 4 per cent between 1970 and 1986 – the only one of the five industries to do so – lower costs and higher allocations to research and innovation suggest a recovery may be in prospect.

Prices of textile products rose between 1970 and 1980 by 60 per cent but, from 1980, there was a steady fall in the prices of exported goods. Domestic prices were maintained until 1985 and then fell sharply. The high relative costs shown in the cost structure are consistent with these prices, and with the report that production capacity had fallen 8 per cent since 1980[9]. Consumer prices have continued to rise over the whole period.

The aggressive financing was associated with a change in the policy for investment. As will be seen from Table 50 savings were made in disbursements for fixed assets to make room for a doubling of the investment in research and innovation.

Summary

The output of the textile industry in the four countries shows marked contrasts; in fact, the only thing that they have in common is the steady rise prior to 1973 (Figure 21, p.105). The fall in Japanese output between 1979 and 1986 contrasts with the rise in that of West Germany after 1982, and the marked improvement in market share. Output in the United Kingdom increased by 12 per cent in the same period and there was no further drop in market share. Thus as indicated in the 1988 report of Courtalds, 'quality not quantity is driving the group ahead'.

Expenditure on R&D in the UK industry increased from 1982 but has remained lower than in West Germany and Japan (Table 51, p.109). Total investment expenditure in textiles was highest in West Germany and lowest in Japan over the whole period, 1972 to 1985 (Figure 22, p.110).

References to Part II

1. Hachiro Koyama, 'Savings based on social structure', *The Japan Economic Journal*, 1 April 1987.
2. Keith Dickson, 'The influence of the Ministry of Defence funding on semi-conductor research and development in the United Kingdom', *Research Policy*, 12 (1983),

   While much of the fault appears to lie with the semiconductor industry's response to MoD funding of its R&D especially its over-reliance on such external support, the paper also suggests that the structure, 'modus operandi', and funding mechanisms of the MoD department concerned have significantly affected the industry's R&D activities.

3. J. Abegglen and Kaisha Stalk, *The Japanese Corporation: the New Competition in World Business*, Basic Books, New York, 1985.
4. Robert Reich, 'The Knot that ties Western ideas to Japan', *Financial Times*, 12 June 1987.
5. Daniel Jones, *Motor Cars: a Maturing Industry*, Frances Pinter, London, 1983, p.130.
6. Shuji Yamamoto, Director, Industrial Research Department, The Industrial Research Department, The Industrial Bank of Japan Ltd., *Long Range Planning*, 19(1), February 1986.
7. John Cassels, *The Sterling Area: an American Analysis*, Economic Co-operation Administration, Special Mission to the United Kingdom, US Government Printing Office, Washington DC, 1951, p.597.
8. *Cotton Industry Working Party Report*, HMSO, London, 1946.
9. Bank of Japan, *Economic Statistics Monthly*, February 1987, Table 103.

Tables and figures to Part II

Table 8 Pattern of costs in mechanical engineering in the United Kingdom: as a percentage of the value of sales

	Norm	1968	1972	1974	1977	1978	1981	1982	1983	1984	1985
For current output	86	87	88	97	90	89	86	88	90	88	88
Materials	40	44	44	51	45	44	40	41	43	43	44
Employment	32	30	32	32	31	31	32	31	31	30	29
Industrial services	4	5	4	6	5	5	4	5	5	4	4
Other services	6	2	3	3	5	5	6	6	6	6	6
Interest payments	2	1	1	2	1	1	2	2	2	2	2
Taxation	2	5	3	3	3	3	2	3	3	3	3
Disposable funds	14	13	12	4	10	11	14	12	10	12	12
Other funds	4	4	3	2	6	7	7	4	4	7	6
Available funds	18	16	15	6	16	18	21	17	15	19	18
For investment	10	10	8	8	9	9	10	10	9	11	10
R&D and innovation	6	6	4	4	4	4	5	5	5	6	5
Fixed capital	4	4	4	4	5	5	4	4	4	5	4
Surplus/deficit	8	6	8	-2	7	9	12	7	5	8	9

Source: *Report on the Census of Production*; Business Monitors, MA3, MA4, MQ14, *Inland Revenue Statistics*

Table 9   Mechanical engineering in the United Kingdom: summary of economic variables

	Index of output 1962=100	As a percentage of the value of sales								Employment (000s)		% unemployment	Trade
		Value added	Total invest-ment	R&D	Fixed capital	Current costs	Material costs	Employ-ment costs	Taxation	Total	R&D	% unem-ployment	Import pene-tration
Era of Ministry of Technology													
1963	99.1	54	9.3	1.43	4.1	85	40	32	5.5	909.8	14.0	1.6	16
1967	123.2	52	10.8	1.71	4.7	85	41	30	5.0	920.0	19.0	1.7	20
1968	128.3	52	10.3	1.53	4.3	84	41		5.0	966.1	17.7	2.1	22
1969	135.3	51	9.7	1.22	4.6	87	41		4.7	1,014.0	15.3	1.7	22
The customer-contractor policy (a)													
1970	139.5	45	8.4	0.83	4.5	92	48	30	3.9	1,032.8	14.0	1.9	20
1971	136.7	46	8.0	0.84	4.1	90	45	32	3.3	992.9	10.5	3.4	17
1972	131.2	49	7.9	0.83	3.9	88	47	32	3.2	887.0	9.7	2.3	24
1973 (oil price shock)	142.7	45	7.8	0.89	3.8	92	47	32	2.9	900.0	9.7	2.3	24
1974	148.7	40	8.3	0.91	4.2	97	51	32	2.5	951.4	10.0	1.9	27
Era of Price Commission (b)													
1975	147.0	46	7.7	0.86	3.8	89	45	32	2.1	916.1	10.5	3.4	25
1976	140.2	46	8.0	0.86	4.1	90	45	32	2.5	906.1	10.6	4.3	30
1977	138.2	44	8.7	0.88	4.6	90	45	31	2.6	912.9	10.9	4.1	31
1978	135.8	46	9.3	0.98	4.9	89	44	31	2.5	889.8	11.4	4.1	30
1979	131.1	48	9.4	1.07	4.9	87	44	31	2.5	955.2	13.1	3.6	30
Post price control (c)													
1980	120.4	50	9.4	1.23	4.6	88	43	33	2.0	900.6	12.9	4.9	29
1981	107.4	51	9.5	1.38	4.2	86	40	32	2.3	799.9	13.1	11.0	30
1982	109.0	48	9.5	1.40	4.3	88	41	31	2.7	725.4	12.4	12.4	33
1983	104.6	46	9.4	1.41	4.2	90	43	31	2.8	672.6	11.6	12.4	36
1984	105.2	47	10.5	1.66	4.5	88	43	30	3.0	552.9	10.9	..	39
1985	116.1	46	9.6	1.50	4.4	88	44	29	3.0	539.9	10.1	..	41

(a) Appendix F, p.164
(b) Counter-Inflation Act 1973 and Price Commission Act 1977
(c) Appendix D, p.157; Competition Act April 1980.

Table 10   Mechanical engineering: wholesale price indices of materials, home sales and exports (1970 = 100)

| | United Kingdom | | West Germany | | |
	Materials	Home sales	Materials	Home sales	Exports
1971	108	111	106	108	108
1972	113	118	107	112	111
1973	128	126	114	118	117
1974	175	154	132	129	128
1975	208	197	142	140	140
1976	252	231	146	147	146
1977	292	269	147	154	153
1978	321	301	150	159	157
1979	357	337	154	165	162
1980	399	387	162	172	171
1981	421	419	175	181	178
1982	453	454	190	191	187
1983	468	482	187	197	193
1984	500	504	189	202	198
1985	530	536	196	208	205
1986	531	560	199	217	213
1987	546	582	195	219	214

Source: *British Business*: Department of Trade and Industry, *Preise und Preisindizes für gewerbliche Produkte*, Reihe 2, Statistisches Bundesamt, Wiesbaden, and calculations by VDMA

Figure 4   Mechanical engineering: index of output (1970 = 100)

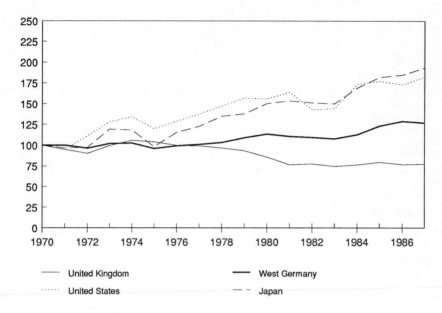

Figure 5   Mechanical engineering: investment

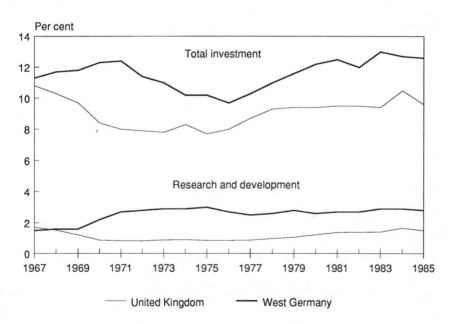

Table 11   Pattern of costs in mechanical engineering in West Germany: as a percentage of the value of sales

	Norm	1972	1975	1977	1981	1982	1983	1984	1985
For current output	86	83	91	94	94	92	90	90	88
Materials	40	38	38	42	41	42	41	42	42
Employment	32	31	36	36	35	33	33	31	30
Industrial services	4	3	4	4	4	4	4	4	4
Other services	6	5	8	8	9	9	9	8	8
Interest	2	2	2	2	2	3	2	2	2
Taxation	2	2	2	3	2	2	2	2	3
Disposable funds	14	18	9	6	6	8	10	10	12
Other funds	4	6	7	6	8	8	7	8	7
Available funds	18	24	16	12	14	16	17	19	19
For investment	10	11	10	10	13	12	13	13	13
R&D and innovation	6	7	7	7	8	8	8	8	8
Fixed capital	4	5	3	4	5	4	5	4	5
Surplus/deficit	8	13	6	2	1	4	4	6	7
Value added	50	53	50	46	46	46	47	46	46
Debts									
Total		52	55	48	53	51	49	48	46
Short-term		36	42	37	42	40	38	37	35
Long-term		16	13	11	11	11	12	11	10

Table 12   Pattern of costs in mechanical engineering in the United States: as a percentage of the value of sales

	Norm	1972	1974	1977	1978	1981	1982	1983	1984	1985
For current output	86	94	94	93	93	94	92	97	98	97
Materials	40	41	44	43	44	43	36	41	41	41
Employment	32	32	31	30	29	29	32	31	30	30
Industrial services	4	2	2	3	3	3	3	3	3	3
Other services	6	12	10	9	9	11	13	13	16	16
Interest payments	2	2	2	2	2	3	4	4	4	4
Taxation	2	6	5	6	6	6	4	4	4	4
Disposable funds	1	6	7	8	7	6	8	3	2	3
Other funds	4	7	6	6	6	8	9	8	6	6
Available funds	18	12	12	14	13	14	17	11	8	9
For investment	10	8	8	8	8	9	10	8	8	9
R&D and innovation	6	4	4	4	4	5	5	5	5	5
Fixed capital	8	4	4	4	4	4	5	3	4	4
Surplus/deficit	8	5	3	6	5	4	7	3	–	–

Source: US Department of Commerce: Bureau of the Census and Bureau of Economic Analysis
National Science Foundation, US Department of the Treasury: Internal Revenue Services

Table 13   Interest payments in mechanical engineering in the United States

	As percentage of: the value of sales	value added	Central Bank discount rates (per cent per annum)
1977	1.9	4.1	6.0
1978	1.9	4.4	9.5
1979	2.2	5.1	12.0
1980	2.8	6.4	13.0
1981	3.3	7.5	12.0
1982	4.0	8.4	8.5
1983	3.9	9.8	8.5
1984	3.9	9.8	8.0
1985	3.9	9.7	7.5

Source: US Department of the Treasury: Internal Revenue Service

Table 14   Direct and indirect tax payments in mechanical engineering in the United States: as a percentage of the value of sales

	1977	1978	1979	1980	1981	1982	1983	1984
Total	6.39	6.29	5.98	5.18	5.35	4.30	4.30	4.35
Indirect	2.73	2.63	2.69	2.64	2.59	2.74	3.08	3.03
Direct	3.66	3.66	3.29	2.54	2.76	1.56	1.22	1.32

Source: US Department of the Treasury: Internal Revenue Service

Table 15   Investment expenditure in mechanical engineering in the United States: as a percentage of the value of sales

	1977	1978	1979	1980	1981	1982	1983	1984	1985
Total	8.0	8.3	8.2	9.0	9.2	9.9	7.8	8.4	8.6
R&D	1.2	1.2	1.2	1.4	1.5	1.8	1.8	1.8	1.7
Innovation	2.4	2.4	2.2	2.5	2.7	3.1	2.6	2.7	2.7
Licensing	0.5	0.6	0.3	0.5	0.5	0.4	0.4	0.4	0.5
Fixed capital	3.9	4.1	4.4	4.6	4.5	4.6	3.0	3.5	3.7

Source: National Science Foundation and US Department of Commerce: Bureau of the Census

Table 16 Pattern of costs in mechanical engineering in Japan: expressed as a percentage of the value of sales

	Norm	1972	1975	1977	1981	1982	1983	1984	1985
For current output	86	96	96	95	93	92	93	94	95
Materials	40	43	44	46	47	45	46	46	45
Employment	32	20	21	20	18	18	18	19	19
Industrial services	4	11	10	11	13	13	13	11	11
Other services	6	15	14	11	9	10	10	14	15
Interest	2	4	5	4	3	3	3	3	2
Taxes	2	3	3	3	3	3	3	3	3
Disposable funds	14	4	4	5	7	8	8	6	5
Other funds	4	4	3	3	3	3	3	3	3
Available funds	18	8	8	8	10	11	11	9	8
For investment	10	7	7	7	8	9	9	8	9
R&D and innovation	6	3	3	4	4	4	5	4	4
Fixed capital	4	4	3	3	4	4	4	4	4
Surplus/deficit	8	1	1	1	2	2	2	1	-1

Source: Census of Manufactures, Yearbook of Labour Statistics, Report on The Survey of Research and Development, Economic Statistics Annual

Table 17 Indices of output and prices for mechanical engineering in Japan (1975 = 100)

		Price indices				
	Index of output	Raw materials	Imported	Products: Exported	Domestic	Yen per $
1974	126	95	95	95	98	308
1975	100	100	100	100	100	308
1976	110	108	107	99	100	308
1977	117	106	112	97	102	234
1978	128	92	118	93	103	206
1979	145	113	127	97	104	242
1980	158	159	140	100	109	210
1981	161	162	141	99	110	233
1982	159	174	166	102	110	237
1983	153	160	161	97	110	231
1984	173	155	154	96	100	254
1985	188	151	163	96	111	231
1986	190	101	129	87	110	185
1987	197	94	120	82	108	177

Source: MITI and Statistical Yearbook for Japan, *Economic Statistics Annual*, The Bank of Japan

Table 18   Employment costs and work put out to contract in mechanical engineering in Japan: expressed as a percentage of the value of sales

	1977	1978	1979	1980	1981	1982	1983	1984	1985
Total	31.2	30.6	30.7	31.0	30.5	30.4	30.8	29.5	29.6
Employment costs	20.2	20.1	18.9	18.1	17.5	17.8	18.4	18.8	18.5
Contract services	11.0	11.5	11.8	12.9	13.0	12.6	12.5	10.7	11.1

Source: Census of Manufactures

Table 19   Expenditure on services in mechanical engineering in Japan: expressed as a percentage of the value of sales

	1977	1978	1979	1980	1981	1982	1983	1984	1985
Total services	22.4	21.8	22.7	22.1	22.3	22.8	22.4	24.2	25.8
Contract services	11.0	11.5	11.8	12.9	13.0	12.6	12.5	10.7	11.1
Other services	11.4	10.3	10.9	9.2	9.3	10.2	9.9	13.5	14.7

Table 20 Mechanical engineering in Japan: summary of economic variables

| | Index of output 1970=100 | As a percentage of the value of sales | | | | | | | | | Employment (000s) | | Trade |
		Value added	Total invest-ment	R&D	Fixed capital	Current costs	Material costs	Employ-ment costs	Interest pay-ments	Taxation	Total	R&D	Import pene-tration
1972	97	31.4	7.0	0.97	4.0	95.5	43.2	20.1	3.82	2.94	1113.30	21.8	3.2
1973	119	31.1	6.9	0.95	4.0	94.4	47.0	19.1	3.44	3.01	983.48	21.7	3.7
1974	118	32.4	7.9	1.28	4.5	94.1	47.7	19.0	4.10	3.36	1133.24	27.7	4.4
1975	98	32.4	6.5	1.11	3.3	95.6	43.6	20.5	4.50	2.97	1058.59	27.9	4.4
1976	115	32.2	5.9	1.21	2.7	96.9	44.6	22.1	4.20	2.82	1037.53	23.1	3.8
1977	123	31.2	6.8	1.67	2.8	95.4	46.4	20.2	3.68	2.66	728.03	25.8	3.5
1978	135	32.1	6.6	1.48	2.9	93.7	46.1	20.1	2.90	2.79	707.51	25.3	3.2
1979	138	30.4	6.8	1.51	3.1	94.4	46.9	18.9	2.47	3.40	703.56	24.9	3.9
1980	150	28.8	7.5	1.58	3.8	95.6	49.2	18.1	2.88	3.44	710.42	26.3	4.1
1981	153	30.8	7.9	1.56	4.0	93.1	46.9	17.5	2.92	3.48	721.96	26.5	3.5
1982	151	31.8	8.5	1.77	4.2	91.9	45.4	17.8	2.62	3.30	726.48	27.4	4.0
1983	150	31.8	8.6	1.92	4.0	92.5	45.8	18.4	2.89	3.06	736.48	29.9	3.6
1984	169	30.2	8.0	1.55	3.8	94.4	45.5	18.8	2.60	3.19	1070.99	32.6	3.8
1985	182	29.1	8.9	1.63	4.4	95.0	45.2	18.5	2.41	3.14	1109.52	33.3	3.9

Source: Census of Manufactures, Statistical Yearbook for Japan, Economic Statistics Annual of the Bank of Japan; OECD Directorate for Science, Technology and Industry

Table 21 Investment expenditure in mechanical engineering: as a percentage of the value of sales

	1972	1973	1974	1975	1976	1977	1978	1979	1980	1981	1982	1983	1984	1985
United Kingdom														
Total investment	7.9	7.8	8.3	7.7	8.0	8.7	9.3	9.4	9.4	9.5	9.5	9.4	10.5	9.6
R&D	0.8	0.9	0.9	0.9	0.9	0.9	1.0	1.1	1.2	1.4	1.4	1.4	1.7	1.5
Innovation*	3.1	3.1	3.1	3.0	3.0	3.2	3.4	3.4	3.5	4.7	3.8	3.8	4.3	3.7
Fixed capital	3.9	3.8	4.2	3.8	4.1	4.6	4.9	4.9	4.6	4.2	4.3	4.2	4.5	4.4
West Germany														
Total investment	11.4	11.0	10.2	10.2	9.7	10.3	11.0	11.6	12.2	12.5	12.0	13.0	12.7	12.6
R&D	2.8	2.9	2.9	3.0	2.7	2.5	2.6	2.8	2.6	2.7	2.7	2.9	2.9	2.8
Innovation*	3.9	4.0	3.8	4.0	4.2	4.1	4.3	4.7	4.9	5.3	5.2	5.5	5.5	5.3
Fixed capital	4.7	4.1	3.5	3.2	2.8	3.6	3.8	4.1	4.7	4.5	4.1	4.6	4.3	4.6
United States														
Total investment	7.5	7.3	8.0	7.9	7.7	8.0	8.3	8.2	9.0	9.2	9.9	7.8	8.4	8.6
R&D	1.3	1.2	1.2	1.2	1.2	1.2	1.2	1.2	1.4	1.5	1.8	1.8	1.8	1.7
Innovation*	2.6	2.7	2.7	2.7	2.9	2.9	3.0	2.5	3.0	3.2	3.5	3.0	3.1	3.2
Fixed capital	3.6	3.3	4.2	4.0	3.6	3.9	4.1	4.4	4.6	4.5	4.6	3.0	3.5	3.7
Japan														
Total investment	7.0	6.9	7.9	6.5	5.9	6.8	6.6	6.8	7.5	7.9	8.5	8.6	8.0	8.9
R&D	1.0	1.0	1.3	1.1	1.2	1.7	1.5	1.5	1.6	1.6	1.8	1.9	1.6	1.6
Innovation*	2.1	2.0	2.2	2.0	2.0	2.3	2.2	2.2	2.2	2.3	2.6	2.8	2.6	2.8
Fixed capital	4.0	4.0	4.5	3.3	2.7	2.8	2.9	3.1	3.8	4.0	4.2	4.0	3.8	4.4

* Includes licence payments

Figure 6   Electronics in the four countries: sales and value added, 1984

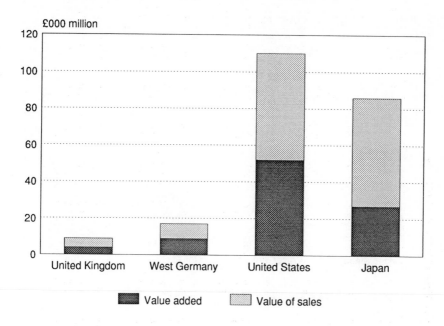

Value added   Value of sales

Figure 7   Electronics in the four countries: employment, 1984

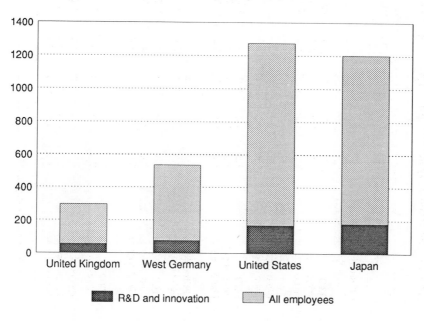

R&D and innovation   All employees

Figure 8   Investment in relation to sales, 1984

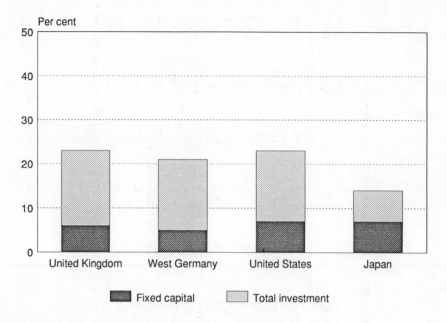

Figure 9   Investment in relation to value added, 1984

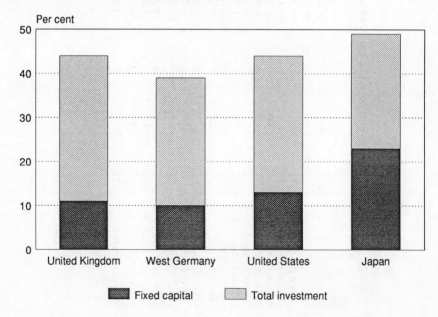

Table 22   Pattern of costs in the electronics industry in the United Kingdom: as a percentage of the value of sales

	Norm	1972	1973	1977	1980	1981	1982	1983	1984	1985
For current output	74	68.2	84.3	82.2	75.9	73.0	71.1	74.0	76.4	72.0
Materials	38	35.2	46.9	43.1	38.1	36.3	36.2	39.2	42.8	42.8
Employment costs	25	25.6	27.3	28.0	28.3	26.7	24.9	23.9	22.6	20.9
Industrial services	3	1.2	2.5	2.5	3.4	3.5	3.2	3.5	3.3	3.0
Other services	2	1.7	0.9	2.1	1.5	1.4	1.3	2.1	2.0	0.3
Interest payments	2	1.5	1.4	1.3	2.0	1.7	1.5	1.2	1.3	1.3
Indirect taxes	1	0.5	0.5	0.7	0.6	0.7	0.6	0.6	0.6	0.5
Direct taxes	3	2.5	4.7	4.5	2.0	2.8	3.3	3.5	3.2	3.2
Disposable funds	26	31.8	15.7	17.8	24.1	27.0	29.0	26.0	23.7	28.0
Other funds	6	4.3	4.8	5.0	6.0	5.0	5.6	6.5	5.8	4.5
Available funds	32	36.1	20.4	22.9	30.0	32.0	34.5	32.4	29.4	32.5
For investment	20	14.8	14.9	18.3	23.3	24.8	24.1	23.6	23.0	25.6
R&D and innovation*	15	11.4	11.0	14.2	18.7	20.1	19.5	18.7	17.4	20.8
Fixed capital	5	3.4	3.9	4.1	4.6	4.8	4.6	4.9	5.7	4.9
Surplus/deficit	12	21.3	5.5	4.5	6.7	7.1	10.5	8.8	6.4	6.8

* Design, product development, market intelligence, planning, industrial engineering and manufacturing start-up. Includes licence payments

Table 23   Value added and gross earnings in the electronics industry: as a percentage of
the value of sales

	1977	1982	1983	1984	1985
Value added					
United Kingdom	52	59	55	52	54
West Germany	56	56	57	54	54
United States	56	55	55	52	53
Japan	29	29	32	28	28
Gross earnings					
United Kingdom	57	64	61	57	57
West Germany	65	67	68	64	62
United States	63	64	65	63	64
Japan	49	50	51	48	49

Table 24   Pattern of costs in the electronics industry in the United Kingdom,
West Germany, the United States and Japan in 1984: as a percentage of
the value of sales

	Norm	United Kingdom	West Germany	United States	Japan
For current output	74	76.4	85.5	83.4	88.1
Materials	38	42.8	36.5	36.6	51.8
Employment costs	25	22.6	35.1	28.0	11.0
Industrial services	3	3.3	2.6	2.4	8.8
Other services	2	2.0	7.0	8.9	11.0
Interest payments	2	1.3	1.5	3.2	1.3
Taxes	4	3.8	2.8	4.5	4.2
Disposable funds	26	23.7	14.5	16.6	11.9
Other funds	6	5.8	11.0	9.2	2.6
Available funds	32	29.4	25.5	25.8	14.4
For investment	20	23.0	21.2	22.8	14.0
R&D and innovation	15	17.4	15.9	15.8	7.4
Fixed capital	5	5.7	5.3	6.9	6.6
Surplus/deficit*	12	6.4	4.3	3.0	0.5

*   Before short-term borrowing, or payments to shareholders, working proprietors, overseas
investment etc.

Table 25 Investment expenditure in the electronics industry: as a percentage of the value of sales

	1972	1973	1974	1975	1976	1977	1978	1979	1980	1981	1982	1983	1984	1985
United Kingdom														
Total investment	14.8	14.9	16.2	14.8	15.1	18.3	22.3	22.9	23.3	24.8	24.1	23.6	23.0	25.6
R&D	9.5	9.1	9.6	8.9	9.5	12.0	14.5	15.4	16.1	17.2	16.6	15.9	14.4	17.9
Innovation	1.9	1.9	2.0	2.1	2.0	2.3	2.6	2.6	2.6	2.9	2.8	2.8	3.0	2.9
Fixed capital	3.4	3.9	4.6	3.9	3.7	4.1	5.2	5.0	4.6	4.8	4.6	4.9	5.7	4.9
West Germany														
Total investment	..	..	..	16.3	19.0	17.4	19.9	20.1	20.3	20.8	21.4	21.0	21.2	24.2
R&D	..	..	..	9.3	10.4	9.2	11.0	11.0	11.2	11.5	12.1	11.6	11.4	12.7
Innovation	..	..	..	3.8	4.2	3.8	4.4	4.3	4.4	4.5	4.7	4.5	4.5	4.8
Fixed capital	..	..	..	3.2	4.5	4.4	4.5	4.7	4.8	4.9	4.6	4.9	5.3	6.5
United States														
Total investment	18.8	18.2	17.9	17.0	16.7	15.7	16.5	17.8	19.1	20.0	20.6	20.6	22.8	23.6
R&D	11.4	10.0	9.4	9.7	9.2	8.2	8.3	8.7	8.9	9.9	9.6	10.5	10.6	11.1
Innovation	4.7	4.3	4.1	4.2	4.0	3.8	3.7	3.9	3.9	4.3	4.8	4.5	5.3	5.6
Fixed capital	2.6	3.8	4.4	3.2	3.4	3.6	4.5	5.2	6.3	5.8	6.3	5.6	6.9	6.9
Japan														
Total investment	8.9	11.3	10.4	9.8	10.3	9.7	9.7	10.4	11.9	12.4	13.5	13.1	14.0	15.0
R&D	3.3	3.3	3.7	4.0	3.7	3.3	3.6	3.8	4.1	4.1	4.5	4.6	4.2	4.8
Innovation	2.9	4.3	3.0	3.2	2.8	2.8	2.9	2.9	3.2	3.0	3.4	3.5	3.2	3.6
Fixed capital	2.7	3.7	3.7	2.6	3.8	3.6	3.2	3.7	4.7	5.3	5.5	5.0	6.6	6.6

Table 26 Pattern of costs in the motor vehicle industry in the United Kingdom: as a percentage of the value of sales

	Norm	1963	1973	1974	1975	1976	1977	1978	1979	1980	1981	1982	1983	1984	1985
For current output	84	87.8	97.7	93.3	99.3	100.8	98.6	95.9	97.7	100.2	99.7	97.8	90.7	94.1	92.2
Materials	50	61.1	62.3	56.0	63.5	62.2	58.7	56.2	58.5	56.3	56.1	57.0	55.3	58.1	57.7
Employment	22	21.0	28.0	28.6	27.6	29.2	29.4	29.4	30.2	33.2	32.5	29.2	25.5	25.4	23.8
Industrial services	2	1.8	1.7	1.7	1.5	1.7	1.9	1.9	1.0	1.1	1.0	1.7	1.6	1.7	1.9
Other services	6	1.7	1.9	2.5	2.6	2.9	3.3	3.7	4.6	5.7	6.2	6.1	5.3	5.9	6.1
Interest payments	2	1.5	1.6	2.4	2.5	2.2	1.6	1.6	2.0	2.8	2.6	2.2	2.0	1.9	1.7
Indirect taxes	1	0.4	0.5	0.8	0.8	0.8	0.8	0.7	0.7	0.9	1.1	1.1	1.0	1.0	0.9
Direct taxes	1	0.4	1.7	1.4	0.8	1.8	2.9	2.3	0.6	0.3	0.3	0.7	–	–	0.1
Disposable funds	16	12.2	2.3	6.7	0.7	-0.8	1.4	4.1	2.3	-0.2	0.3	2.2	9.3	5.9	7.8
Other funds	8	1.9	2.9	2.2	4.4	9.1	7.6	11.4	6.4	16.3	20.6	12.8	8.0	9.8	9.2
Available funds	24	14.1	5.2	8.9	5.2	8.4	8.9	15.5	8.7	16.1	20.9	15.0	17.3	15.8	17.0
For investment	12	8.1	7.7	8.2	7.1	7.3	8.2	9.0	11.5	11.4	10.2	11.4	12.0	13.1	12.6
R&D and innovation	8	3.7	3.9	3.7	3.7	3.7	3.9	3.6	3.9	4.4	4.8	6.0	6.0	7.4	7.7
Fixed capital	4	4.4	3.8	4.5	3.4	3.6	4.3	5.4	7.6	7.0	5.4	5.3	6.0	5.7	4.8
Surplus/deficit	12	6.1	-2.5	0.6	-1.9	1.1	0.7	6.4	-2.8	4.7	10.7	3.6	5.3	2.7	5.9

Figure 10 Motor vehicles: index of output (1970 = 100)

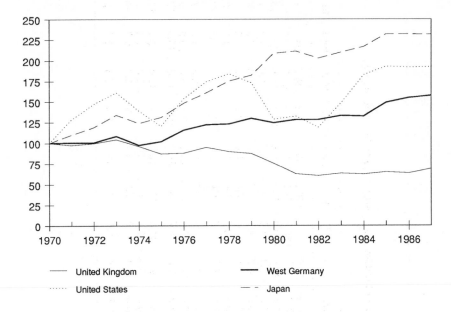

— United Kingdom   ▬ West Germany

····· United States   – – Japan

Figure 11 Motor vehicles: research and development expenditure

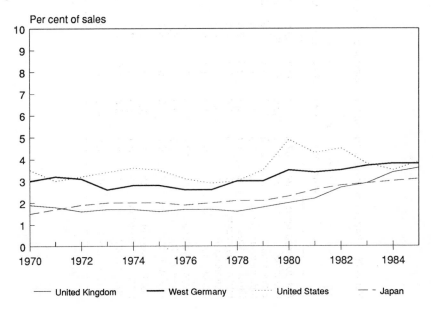

— United Kingdom   ▬ West Germany   ····· United States   – – Japan

Figure 12   Motor vehicles: index of output (1958 = 100)

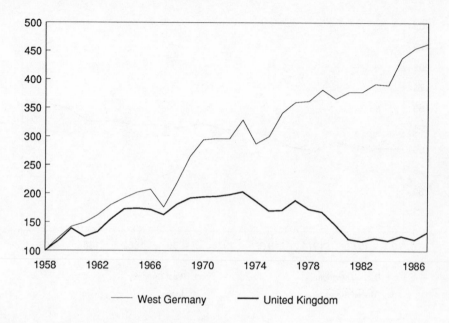

Figure 13   Motor vehicles: total investment expenditure

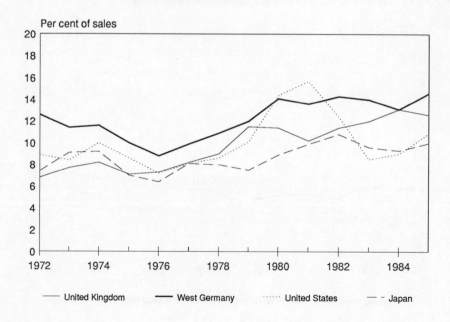

Table 27   Support from government for the motor vehicle industry in the United Kingdom

£ million

	1978	1979	1980	1981	1982	1983	1984
Total	193.3	167.2	345.5	567.2	404.0	119.0	32.5
Selective investment schemes	3.3	3.2	1.5	1.7	3.7	3.5	4.5
Regional development grants	16.0	14.0	44.0	45.5	40.3	25.5	28.0
Finance for British Leyland	174.0	150.0	300.0	520.0	380.0	90.0	–

Source: *The Government's Expenditure Plans 1985-86 to 1987-88*, Cmnd 9428-11, HM Treasury, January 1985

Table 28   Motor vehicles in the United Kingdom: summary of economic variables

	Index of output 1970=100	As a percentage of the value of sales								Employment (000s)		Trade	
		Value added	Total invest-ment	R&D	Fixed capital	Current costs	Material costs	Interest pay-ments	Taxation	Total	R&D	Import pene-tration	Market share
Era of Ministry of Technology													
1963	80	35.6	8.1	1.6	4.4	87.8	61.1	1.5	0.8	432.8	15.5	3.0	
1964	89	:	8.9	1.6	5.4	:	:	2.0	1.0	457.2	15.6		
1966	89	:	11.6	2.2	6.7	:	:	2.0	1.5	472.0	16.2		
1967	84	35.0	11.3	2.2	6.5	91.2	61.5	2.7	2.3	456.0	14.2	6.0	
1968	94	:	7.3	1.9	3.3	:	:	1.7	1.9	455.5	14.4		
1969	99	:	7.8	1.9	3.6	:	:	2.2	2.2	471.0	14.1		
The customer-contractor policy (a)													
1970	100	28.0	9.6	1.9	5.5	98.3	68.6	1.9	0.9	484.3	14.0	8.1	10.1
1971	101	30.3	8.4	1.8	4.4	96.0	66.0	1.5	1.1	481.4	13.5	11.3	9.9
1972	102	36.1	6.8	1.6	2.5	92.1	61.2	1.3	1.0	478.8	13.4	17.6	8.2
1973 (oil price shock)	105	34.1	7.7	1.7	3.8	97.7	62.3	1.6	2.2	491.1	13.5	20.3	7.5
1974	97	39.8	8.2	1.7	4.5	93.3	56.0	2.4	2.2	500.3	14.0	20.3	7.2
Era of Price Commission (b)													
1975	87	32.4	7.1	1.6	3.4	99.3	63.5	2.5	1.6	480.0	14.4	25.5	7.6
1976	88	33.2	7.3	1.7	3.6	100.8	62.2	2.2	2.6	470.6	13.8	28.8	6.6
1977	95	36.1	8.2	1.7	4.3	98.6	58.7	1.6	3.7	492.4	13.3	34.8	6.5
1978	89	38.2	9.0	1.6	5.4	95.9	56.2	1.6	3.0	494.7	12.3	36.4	6.4
1979	87	35.9	11.5	1.8	7.6	97.7	58.5	2.0	1.3	489.5	12.8	41.9	6.2
Post price control (c)													
1980	75	36.9	11.4	2.0	7.0	100.2	56.3	2.8	1.2	447.6	11.2	40.8	6.3
1981	62	36.8	10.2	2.2	5.4	99.7	56.1	2.6	1.4	368.7	9.7	43.9	5.3
1982	60	35.3	11.4	2.7	5.3	97.8	57.0	2.2	1.8	324.8	10.8	49.0	4.8
1983	63	37.8	12.0	3.1	6.0	90.7	55.3	2.0	1.0	301.8	10.5	53.5	3.9
1984	61	34.2	13.1	3.4	5.7	94.1	58.1	1.9	1.0	288.1	13.7	51.3	3.4
1985	65	34.3	12.6	3.6	4.8	92.2	57.7	1.7	0.9	276.1	13.2	51.3	3.5

Source: Census of Production (annual from 1970), R&D Survey: Department of Trade and Industry; OECD Directorate for Science,
          Technology and Industry

(a) Appendix F, p.164
(b) Prices Act 1974 and the Price Commission Act 1977
(c) Appendix D, p.157; Competition Act 1980

Table 29 Pattern of costs in the motor vehicle industry in West Germany: as a percentage of the value of sales

	Norm	1975	1977	1980	1981	1982	1983	1984	1985
For current output	84	90.4	93.4	94.4	92.6	91.6	90.9	92.6	89.5
Materials	50	49.5	51.1	48.6	48.7	49.7	49.6	50.5	41.8
Employment	22	29.1	28.7	32.9	30.4	29.1	28.9	28.9	30.2
Industrial services	6	2.6	2.9	3.4	3.3	3.4	3.5	3.6	4.0
Other services	2	5.3	4.8	5.5	5.7	5.3	4.9	5.5	8.1
Interest payments	2	1.2	0.8	1.0	1.4	1.2	0.8	0.8	0.7
Taxes	2	2.8	5.1	3.0	3.1	3.0	3.1	3.2	3.7
Disposable funds	16	9.6	6.6	5.6	7.4	8.4	9.1	7.4	10.5
Other funds	8	5.2	7.1	7.6	7.8	8.8	8.7	9.8	8.4
Available funds	24	14.8	13.7	13.1	15.2	17.2	17.8	17.2	18.9
For investment	12	10.0	9.9	14.1	13.6	14.3	14.0	13.1	14.6
R&D and innovation	8	5.8	5.4	7.1	6.9	7.1	7.3	7.5	8.6
Fixed capital	4	4.1	4.5	7.0	6.7	7.2	6.7	5.7	6.1
Surplus/deficit	12	4.8	3.8	-1.0	1.6	2.9	3.9	4.1	4.2

Table 30 Investment in the motor vehicle industry in West Germany: as a percentage of the value of sales

	1972	1975	1977	1980	1981	1982	1983	1984	1985
Total investment	12.6	10.0	9.9	14.1	13.6	14.3	14.0	13.1	14.6
R&D	2.6	2.8	2.6	3.5	3.4	3.5	3.7	3.8	3.8
Innovation	3.1	3.0	2.7	3.6	3.5	3.5	3.6	3.7	4.8
Fixed capital	6.9	4.1	4.5	7.0	6.7	7.2	6.7	5.7	6.1

Table 31   Pattern of costs in the motor vehicle industry in the United States: as a percentage of the value of sales

	Norm	1972	1975	1977	1979	1980	1981	1982	1983	1984	1985
For current output	84	90.9	95.0	96.9	96.9	98.5	100.6	99.8	96.9	97.2	96.3
Materials	50	64.8	68.1	67.9	67.1	68.2	67.9	67.1	66.8	68.0	67.6
Employment costs	22	15.7	15.0	15.0	15.2	16.2	15.6	15.1	13.0	13.0	12.6
Industrial services	2	0.5	0.5	0.5	0.6	0.6	0.7	0.7	0.7	0.7	0.7
Other services	6	3.0	4.3	4.3	5.1	4.6	5.4	6.1	6.5	5.7	5.5
Interest payments	2	1.5	3.0	2.3	3.8	5.5	6.9	7.2	5.7	5.2	5.2
Taxes	2	5.3	4.1	6.8	5.2	3.3	4.1	3.7	4.2	4.7	4.7
Disposable funds	16	9.1	5.0	3.1	3.1	1.5	-0.6	0.2	3.1	2.8	3.8
Other funds	8	4.2	3.9	6.2	7.9	7.5	9.2	9.9	6.0	7.8	8.5
Available funds	24	13.3	8.9	9.3	11.0	9.0	8.6	10.1	9.1	10.6	12.3
For investment	12	8.9	8.6	8.1	10.1	14.4	15.7	12.4	8.5	9.0	10.9
R&D and innovation	8	6.5	7.1	6.1	7.3	9.7	8.6	9.0	7.9	7.2	8.1
Fixed assets	4	2.5	1.5	1.9	2.8	4.7	7.1	3.4	0.6	1.9	2.9
Surplus/deficit	12	4.4	0.3	1.3	0.9	-5.4	-7.1	-2.3	0.6	1.6	1.4

Table 32   Investment in the motor vehicle industry in the United States

Per cent

	1979	1980	1981	1982	1983	1984	1985
Total investment	10.1	14.4	15.7	12.4	8.5	9.0	10.9
R&D	3.5	4.9	4.3	4.5	3.8	3.5	3.9
Innovation	3.8	4.8	4.3	4.6	4.1	3.6	4.2
Fixed capital	2.8	4.7	7.1	3.4	0.6	1.9	2.8

Source: Census of Manufactures, National Science Foundation

Table 33 Pattern of costs in the motor vehicle industry in Japan: as a percentage of the value of sales

	Norm	1972	1975	1977	1979	1980	1981	1982	1983	1984	1985
For current output	84	92.4	93.6	92.6	91.9	91.6	91.5	89.9	90.7	90.9	89.7
Materials	50	66.4	64.4	63.1	63.6	65.6	65.0	63.6	62.4	63.1	62.9
Employment costs	22	11.5	11.9	11.1	11.0	10.4	9.9	10.3	10.3	10.1	10.0
Industrial services	2	5.5	4.7	4.7	4.5	4.9	4.7	5.5	5.0	5.4	5.2
Other services	6	3.3	6.5	8.4	7.7	6.0	7.4	5.9	8.5	8.4	6.8
Interest payments	2	2.4	3.0	1.7	1.2	1.4	1.2	1.3	1.3	1.2	1.1
Taxes	2	3.2	3.2	3.6	3.8	3.4	3.3	3.3	3.2	2.8	3.8
Disposable funds	16	7.6	6.4	7.4	8.1	8.4	8.5	10.1	9.3	9.1	10.3
Other funds	8	3.3	3.2	2.6	2.2	2.2	2.2	2.3	2.3	2.3	2.3
Available funds	24	10.9	9.6	10.0	10.2	10.6	10.7	12.4	11.6	11.4	12.6
For investment	12	7.4	7.0	8.1	7.5	8.9	9.9	10.8	9.6	9.3	10.0
R&D and innovation	8	4.2	4.5	4.4	4.7	5.0	5.7	6.2	6.2	6.3	6.4
Fixed capital	4	3.2	2.5	3.8	2.8	3.9	4.2	4.5	3.4	3.0	3.6
Surplus/deficit	8	3.5	2.6	1.9	2.7	1.8	0.7	1.6	2.0	2.1	2.6
Dividends paid		0.7	0.5	0.5	0.5	0.5	0.5	0.5	0.5	0.5	0.4

Table 34 Pattern of costs in the motor vehicle industry in the United Kingdom, West Germany, the United States and Japan in 1984: as a percentage of the value of sales

	Norm	United Kingdom	West Germany	United States	Japan
For current output	84	94.1	92.6	97.2	90.9
Materials	50	58.1	50.5	68.0	63.1
Employment	22	25.4	28.9	13.0	10.1
Industrial services	2	1.7	3.6	0.7	5.4
Other services	6	5.9	5.5	5.7	8.4
Interest payments	2	1.9	0.8	5.2	1.2
Indirect taxes	1	1.0	1.3	2.4	0.7
Direct taxes	1	−	1.9	2.4	2.1
Disposable funds	16	5.9	7.4	2.8	9.1
Other funds	8	9.8	9.8	7.8	2.3
Available funds	24	15.8	17.2	10.6	11.4
For investment	12	13.1	13.1	9.0	9.3
R&D and innovation	8	7.4	7.5	7.2	6.3
Fixed capital	4	5.7	5.7	1.9	3.0
Surplus/deficit *	12	2.7	4.1	1.6	2.1
Value added	42	34.3	40.4	25.6	23.1

* Before short-term borrowing, payments to shareholders, working proprietors, overseas investmen etc

Table 35 Investment expenditure in the motor vehicle industry: as a percentage of the value of sales

	1972	1973	1974	1975	1976	1977	1978	1979	1980	1981	1982	1983	1984	1985
United Kingdom														
Total investment	6.8	7.7	8.2	7.1	7.3	8.2	9.0	11.5	11.4	10.2	11.4	12.0	13.1	12.6
R&D	1.6	1.7	1.7	1.6	1.7	1.7	1.6	1.8	2.0	2.2	2.7	2.9	3.4	3.6
Innovation	2.7	2.1	2.0	2.0	2.0	2.1	2.0	2.2	2.4	2.6	3.3	3.1	4.0	4.2
Fixed capital	2.5	3.8	4.5	3.4	3.6	4.3	5.4	7.6	7.0	5.4	5.3	6.0	5.7	4.8
West Germany														
Total investment	12.6	11.4	11.6	10.0	8.8	9.9	10.9	12.0	14.1	13.6	14.3	14.0	13.1	14.6
R&D	2.6	2.6	2.8	2.8	2.6	2.6	3.0	3.0	3.5	3.4	3.5	3.7	3.8	3.8
Innovation	3.1	3.1	3.2	3.0	2.7	2.7	3.1	3.0	3.6	3.5	3.5	3.6	3.7	4.8
Fixed capital	6.9	5.6	5.5	4.1	3.5	4.5	4.9	6.0	7.0	6.7	7.2	6.7	5.7	6.1
United States														
Total investment	8.9	8.4	10.0	8.6	7.2	8.1	8.6	10.1	14.4	15.7	12.4	8.5	9.0	10.9
R&D	3.2	3.4	3.6	3.5	3.1	2.9	3.0	3.5	4.9	4.3	4.5	3.8	3.5	3.9
Innovation	3.3	3.5	3.7	3.6	3.2	3.2	3.3	3.8	4.8	4.3	4.6	4.1	3.6	4.2
Fixed capital	2.5	1.6	2.6	1.5	1.0	1.9	2.3	2.8	4.7	7.1	3.4	0.6	1.9	2.9
Japan														
Total investment	7.4	9.1	9.2	7.0	6.4	8.1	8.0	7.5	8.9	9.9	10.8	9.6	9.3	10.0
R&D	1.9	2.0	2.0	2.0	1.9	2.0	2.1	2.1	2.3	2.6	2.8	2.9	3.0	3.1
Innovation	2.3	2.7	2.4	2.5	2.3	2.4	2.6	2.6	2.6	3.1	3.5	3.3	3.3	3.4
Fixed capital	3.2	4.5	4.7	2.5	2.3	3.8	3.3	2.8	3.9	4.2	4.5	3.4	3.0	3.6

Figure 14   Motor vehicles: fixed capital expenditure

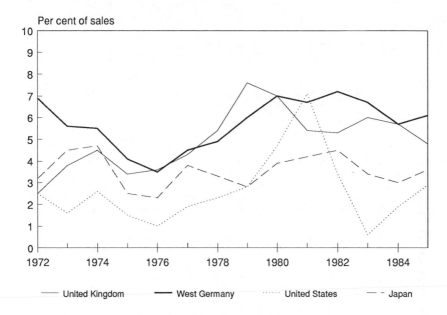

Per cent of sales

Legend: United Kingdom — West Germany — United States — Japan

Figure 15   Motor vehicles: market share of OECD exports

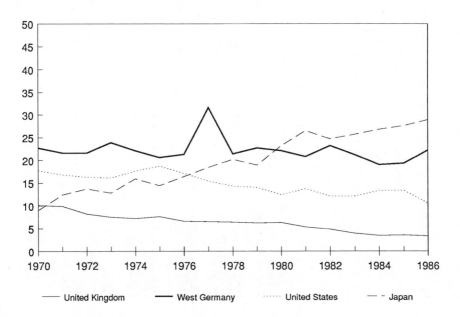

Legend: United Kingdom — West Germany — United States — Japan

Table 36   Pattern of costs in the chemical industry in the United Kingdom: as a percentage of the value of sales

	Norm	1972	1974	1975	1977	1980	1981	1982	1983	1984	1985
For current output	85	78.0	89.1	86.3	84.7	86.0	86.7	86.2	82.3	80.5	80.3
Materials	50	50.2	62.5	57.5	58.9	56.7	57.9	57.2	55.9	56.0	55.8
Employment costs	20	17.1	14.8	17.0	14.6	16.7	16.2	16.0	14.4	13.2	13.0
Industrial services	2	2.0	2.4	2.4	2.4	2.4	2.1	2.4	2.3	2.2	2.1
Other services	8	3.7	4.4	4.6	4.9	5.5	5.9	6.1	5.6	5.8	5.5
Interest payments	2	2.1	2.5	2.4	2.1	2.8	2.8	2.6	2.1	1.5	2.0
Taxes	3	3.0	2.6	2.4	2.0	1.9	1.8	2.0	1.9	2.0	2.0
Disposable funds	15	22.0	10.9	13.7	15.3	14.0	13.3	13.8	17.7	19.5	19.7
Other funds	5	6.8	5.8	6.2	5.7	6.8	6.9	6.1	7.2	10.8	7.7
Available funds	20	28.8	16.7	19.9	21.0	20.8	20.2	19.9	25.0	30.3	27.4
For investment	14	11.4	9.3	12.4	11.5	13.3	12.1	12.1	12.1	11.6	13.2
R&D and innovation	9	5.6	4.7	5.5	5.5	6.6	6.8	7.0	7.3	7.1	7.5
Fixed capital	5	5.7	4.5	6.9	5.9	6.7	5.2	5.0	4.8	4.4	5.7
Surplus/deficit	6	17.4	7.4	7.5	9.4	7.5	8.1	7.8	12.9	18.7	14.2

Table 37   Pattern of costs in the chemical industry in West Germany: as a percentage of the value of sales

	Norm	1975	1977	1979	1980	1981	1982	1983	1984	1985
For current output	85	83.2	88.3	89.6	90.8	90.8	88.9	87.7	88.5	88.6
Materials	50	40.4	45.2	47.8	47.8	49.0	47.3	46.8	48.1	48.2
Employment costs	20	23.8	22.6	21.8	23.0	22.3	22.4	22.2	21.2	21.2
Industrial services	2	3.4	3.9	3.9	4.0	3.7	3.5	3.2	3.3	3.5
Other services	8	10.8	11.7	11.0	11.2	11.4	11.4	11.6	11.7	11.2
Interest payments	2	2.0	1.6	1.3	1.5	1.8	1.6	1.1	0.9	1.0
Taxes	3	2.9	3.5	3.6	3.1	2.4	2.4	2.8	3.3	3.6
Disposable funds	15	16.8	11.7	10.4	9.2	9.2	11.1	12.3	11.5	11.4
Other funds	5	7.6	7.6	6.7	8.2	8.3	8.3	7.9	7.0	8.3
Available funds	20	24.4	19.2	17.1	17.3	17.6	19.5	20.2	18.4	19.7
For investment	14	14.0	13.4	12.5	13.3	13.4	13.3	12.9	12.3	13.2
R&D and innovation	9	7.8	7.8	7.6	8.0	8.4	8.6	8.3	8.0	8.6
Fixed capital	5	6.2	5.6	5.0	5.4	5.1	4.8	4.5	4.2	4.6
Surplus/deficit	6	10.4	5.8	4.7	4.0	4.2	6.2	7.3	6.1	6.5

Table 38 Pattern of costs in the chemical industry in the United States: as a percentage of the value of sales

	Norm	1972	1974	1975	1977	1980	1981	1982	1983	1984	1985
For current output	85	81.1	82.9	83.9	87.1	88.2	89.4	91.8	89.5	90.2	87.1
Materials	50	41.0	46.9	47.6	50.3	52.5	54.2	51.8	50.5	50.5	47.5
Employment costs	20	15.4	12.9	12.8	12.3	11.8	11.3	12.5	12.0	11.4	11.4
Industrial services	2	1.7	1.8	1.9	2.0	1.9	1.9	1.8	1.8	1.8	1.7
Other services	8	15.2	13.1	13.8	14.3	14.3	14.6	17.7	17.5	18.2	18.3
Interest payments	2	1.4	1.5	1.8	1.8	2.4	3.0	3.2	2.9	3.0	3.0
Taxes	3	6.4	6.7	6.1	6.5	5.2	4.5	4.8	4.9	5.3	5.3
Disposable funds	15	18.9	17.1	16.1	12.9	11.8	10.6	8.2	10.5	9.8	12.9
Other funds	5	6.6	7.2	7.4	8.3	8.6	9.4	9.3	9.4	8.4	8.2
Available funds	20	25.5	24.2	23.4	21.2	20.4	20.0	17.5	20.0	18.1	21.0
For investment	14	10.7	11.5	12.9	12.5	11.2	11.5	12.4	10.7	10.7	10.8
R&D and innovation	9	6.3	5.6	5.9	5.5	5.7	6.2	7.2	7.3	6.9	7.3
Fixed capital	5	4.3	5.9	7.1	7.0	5.5	5.3	5.2	3.4	3.8	3.5
Surplus/deficit	6	14.8	12.7	10.5	8.7	9.2	8.5	5.2	9.3	7.4	10.3

Table 39   United States direct investment abroad by the chemical industry and foreign
direct investment

$ million

| | United States direct investment abroad | | Foreign direct investment in United States | |
	Investment	Income	Investment	Income
1982	546	1140	682	247
1983	116	1120	1390	515
1984	242	1206	834	819
1985	782	2320	1945	488
1986	1932	3896	4106	518
1987	4093	5369	8567	1964

Source: US Department of Commerce: *Survey of Current Business*

Table 40   Pattern of costs in the chemical industry in Japan: as a percentage of the value of sales

	Norm	1972	1974	1975	1977	1980	1981	1982	1983	1984	1985
For current output	85	89.4	90.2	92.5	92.3	90.8	91.6	90.7	89.1	88.7	88.8
Materials	50	48.5	58.6	58.6	59.0	63.6	61.5	59.8	57.1	56.5	55.8
Employment costs	20	9.3	9.1	9.7	9.3	7.2	7.5	7.5	7.3	6.9	7.3
Industrial services	2	1.9	2.3	2.3	2.2	2.2	2.2	2.3	2.4	2.4	2.4
Other services	8	22.3	12.7	15.3	15.5	11.6	13.8	15.1	16.2	16.8	17.2
Interest payments	2	4.6	4.1	4.6	3.7	3.3	3.6	3.0	2.9	2.6	2.5
Taxes	3	2.8	3.4	2.0	2.6	3.0	3.0	3.1	3.3	3.5	3.6
Disposable funds	15	10.6	9.8	7.5	7.7	9.2	8.4	9.3	10.9	11.3	11.2
Other funds	5	3.7	3.0	2.8	3.0	2.3	2.4	2.6	2.7	2.6	2.2
Available funds	20	14.3	12.8	10.3	10.7	11.5	10.9	12.0	13.5	13.9	13.4
For investment	14	14.7	11.2	13.8	10.0	9.2	10.1	11.0	11.3	11.0	11.8
R&D and innovation	9	6.2	5.3	5.4	5.4	5.5	6.0	6.6	7.1	7.4	7.9
Fixed capital	5	8.6	5.9	8.5	4.6	3.7	4.1	4.4	4.2	3.6	3.9
Surplus/deficit	6	-0.4	1.5	-3.5	0.7	2.3	0.8	0.9	2.3	2.9	1.6

Table 41   The chemical industry in Japan: producer prices and production capacity (1980 = 100)

	Price indices		Production indices	
	Domestic	Export	Production capacity	Operating rate
1980	100	100	100	100
1981	97	95	102	93
1982	97	101	103	91
1983	95	95	105	94
1984	94	94	106	102
1985	92	93	106	103
1986	85	92	106	103
1987	82	79	107	108

Source: *Economic Statistics Annual*, Bank of Japan

Table 42   Investment expenditure in the chemical industry: as a percentage of the value of sales

	1972	1973	1974	1975	1976	1977	1978	1979	1980	1981	1982	1983	1984	1985
United Kingdom														
Total investment	11.4	9.9	9.3	12.4	11.5	11.5	13.5	12.7	13.3	12.1	12.1	12.1	11.6	13.2
R&D	3.0	2.8	2.6	3.0	2.7	3.0	3.3	3.4	3.8	3.9	3.9	4.1	3.9	4.5
Innovation	2.6	2.4	2.2	2.5	2.4	2.5	2.5	2.6	2.8	2.9	3.1	3.3	3.2	3.0
Fixed capital	5.7	4.6	4.5	6.9	6.4	5.9	7.7	6.7	6.7	5.2	5.0	4.8	4.4	5.7
West Germany														
Total investment	14.7	13.2	12.7	14.0	13.1	13.4	13.5	12.5	13.3	13.4	13.3	12.9	12.3	13.2
R&D	4.6	4.3	4.2	4.6	4.6	4.6	5.0	4.5	4.5	4.7	5.0	5.1	4.8	5.1
Innovation	3.2	3.0	2.9	3.2	3.2	3.2	3.4	3.1	3.3	3.4	3.5	3.3	3.2	3.5
Fixed capital	6.9	5.8	5.6	6.2	5.3	5.6	5.1	5.0	5.4	5.1	4.8	4.5	4.2	4.6
United States														
Total investment	10.7	10.7	11.5	12.9	12.7	12.5	11.7	10.9	11.2	11.5	12.4	10.7	10.7	10.8
R&D	3.6	3.5	3.2	3.3	3.1	2.9	3.0	2.9	3.1	3.3	4.2	4.3	4.3	4.6
Innovation	2.7	2.6	2.4	2.6	2.7	2.6	2.6	2.6	2.7	2.8	3.0	3.1	2.6	2.7
Fixed capital	4.3	4.5	5.9	7.1	6.8	7.0	6.2	5.4	5.5	5.3	5.2	3.4	3.8	3.5
Japan														
Total investment	14.7	10.8	11.2	13.8	11.0	10.0	9.8	9.0	9.2	10.1	11.0	11.3	11.0	11.8
R&D	3.4	3.3	3.2	3.2	3.1	3.2	3.3	3.5	3.3	3.7	4.0	4.4	4.6	4.9
Innovation	2.8	2.3	2.2	2.2	2.0	2.1	2.1	2.3	2.1	2.3	2.5	2.7	2.8	3.0
Fixed capital	8.6	5.2	5.9	8.5	5.8	4.6	4.3	3.2	3.7	4.1	4.4	4.2	3.6	3.9

Table 43 Pattern of costs in the chemical industry in the United Kingdom, West Germany, the United States and Japan in 1985: as a percentage of the value of sales

	Norm	United Kingdom	West Germany	United States	Japan
For current output	85	80.3	88.6	87.1	88.8
Materials	50	55.8	48.2	47.5	55.8
Employment costs	20	13.0	21.2	11.4	7.3
Industrial services	2	2.1	3.5	1.7	2.4
Other services	8	5.5	11.2	18.3	17.2
Interest payments	2	2.0	1.0	3.0	2.5
Indirect taxes	1	0.6	1.5	2.3	1.0
Direct taxes	2	1.3	2.1	3.1	2.7
Disposable funds	15	19.7	11.4	12.9	11.2
Other funds	5	7.7	8.3	8.2	2.2
Available funds	20	27.4	19.7	21.0	13.4
For investment	14	13.2	13.2	10.8	11.8
R&D and innovation	10	7.5	8.6	7.3	7.9
Fixed capital	4	5.7	4.6	3.5	3.9
Surplus/deficit *	6	14.2	6.5	10.3	1.6
Value added	40	36.0	37.1	32.6	24.6

*   Before short-term borrowing, payment to shareholders, working proprietors, overseas investment etc.

Figure 16   Chemicals: total investment expenditure

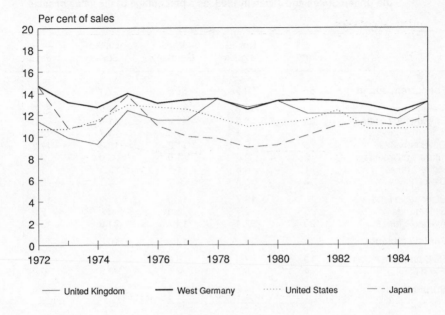

Figure 17   Chemicals: index of output (1970 = 100)

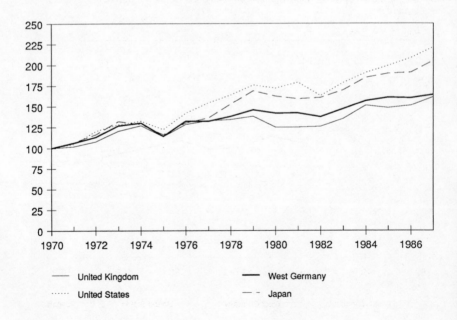

Figure 18 Chemicals: research and development

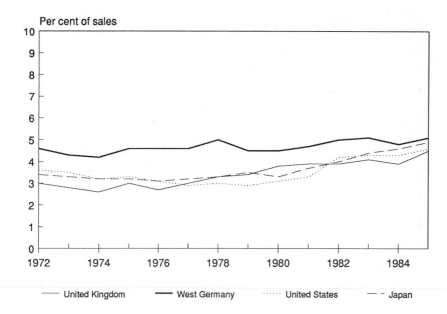

Figure 19 Chemicals: fixed capital expenditure

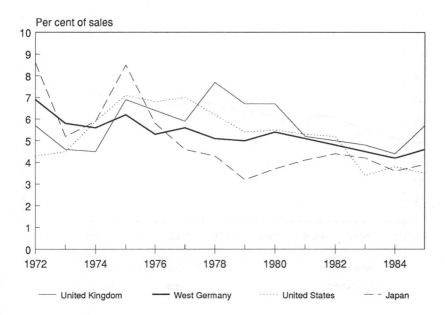

Figure 20   Chemicals: research and development employees

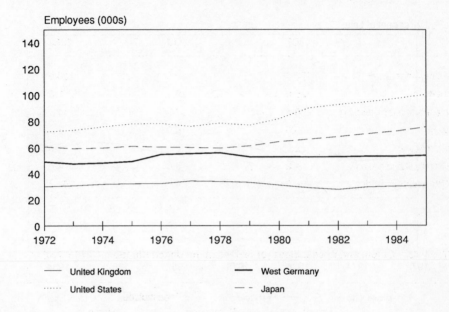

Table 44   Sales of textiles in the United Kingdom: as a percentage of sales of all manufactures

	1907	1970	1980
All manufacturing	100.0	100.0	100.0
Textiles	25.0	8.1	3.2
Mechanical engineering	8.4	13.0	11.4
Vehicles	6.6	10.0	3.6
Chemicals	2.6	5.3	11.6
Electrical engineering	1.2	9.6	8.0
Other manufacturing	56.2	54.0	62.2

Table 45   Output and price indices for textiles in the United Kingdom (1970 = 100)

		Price indices		
	Index of output	Purchased materials	Home sales	
1970	100	100.0	100.0	
1971	99	104.8	104.9	
1972	101	119.0	112.2	+6.8
1973	105	166.7	131.7	+35.0
1974	96	189.9	162.2	+27.7
1975	89	201.7	178.6	+23.1
1976	92	265.5	205.9	+59.6
1977	92	293.2	242.2	+51.0
1978	89	300.2	262.9	+37.3
1979	85	338.4	291.1	+47.3

Table 46   Pattern of costs in the textile industry in the United Kingdom: as a percentage of the value of sales

	Norm	1974	1975	1977	1980	1981	1982	1983	1984	1985
For current output	94	94.0	93.1	93.9	92.7	93.7	94.9	92.3	94.2	91.6
Materials	50	58.1	53.9	57.5	52.2	52.9	53.4	54.0	55.9	55.2
Employment costs	25	24.8	27.5	25.2	28.3	28.3	27.6	26.3	25.6	24.6
Industrial services	4	4.3	4.5	4.5	3.9	3.7	3.6	3.6	3.3	3.6
Other services	9	3.1	3.6	3.6	4.3	4.7	4.7	4.7	4.6	4.5
Interest payments	2	2.2	2.1	1.7	2.4	2.5	3.7	2.2	3.2	1.6
Taxes	4	1.6	1.6	1.4	1.7	1.6	1.9	1.5	1.6	1.9
Disposable funds	6	6.0	6.9	6.1	7.3	6.3	5.1	7.7	5.8	8.4
Other funds	4	3.2	2.3	2.5	2.5	2.9	6.5	6.2	6.7	4.4
Available funds	10	9.2	9.2	8.6	9.8	9.2	11.6	13.9	12.5	12.8
For investment	6	6.0	4.9	4.0	4.6	4.1	4.4	4.5	5.1	5.3
R&D and innovation	2	0.6	0.7	0.5	0.7	0.7	0.8	0.9	0.9	0.8
Fixed capital	2	5.4	4.3	3.5	3.9	3.4	3.7	3.7	4.2	4.5
Surplus/deficit	4	3.2	4.3	4.6	5.2	5.1	7.2	9.4	7.4	7.5

Figure 21 Textiles: index of output (1970 = 100)

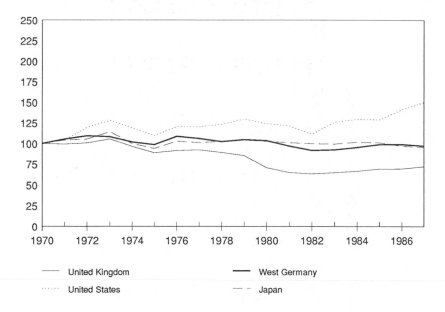

- United Kingdom
- West Germany
.... United States
- - Japan

Table 47 Pattern of costs in the textile industry in West Germany: as a percentage of the value of sales

	Norm	1975	1977	1980	1981	1982	1983	1984	1985
For current output	94	93.9	95.4	97.8	98.4	97.2	97.0	97.0	95.5
Materials	50	45.5	48.3	48.5	48.2	48.0	49.4	50.8	50.3
Employment	25	30.7	30.0	30.4	30.5	29.6	28.7	27.9	26.6
Industrial services	4	6.3	6.7	7.5	7.2	7.2	7.1	7.1	7.4
Other services	9	7.3	6.9	7.2	7.9	7.9	7.9	7.6	7.6
Interest	2	2.2	1.7	2.4	3.0	2.9	2.0	1.8	1.8
Taxes	4	1.8	1.8	1.7	1.6	1.5	1.8	1.7	1.6
Disposable funds	6	6.1	4.6	2.2	1.6	2.8	3.0	3.0	4.5
Other funds	4	6.4	5.9	6.9	6.9	6.6	6.7	5.9	6.1
Available funds	10	12.5	10.5	9.1	8.6	9.3	9.7	9.0	10.7
For investment	6	4.9	5.3	5.8	5.1	5.3	6.3	6.0	6.4
R&D and innovation	2	0.7	0.7	1.0	1.0	1.0	1.1	1.1	1.1
Fixed capital	4	4.2	4.5	4.9	4.1	4.3	5.2	4.9	5.3
Surplus/deficit	4	7.6	5.2	3.3	3.5	4.0	3.4	3.0	4.3

105

Table 48   Pattern of costs in the textile industry in the United States: as a percentage of the value of sales

	Norm	1972	1974	1975	1977	1980	1981	1982	1983	1984	1985
For current output	94	98.8	99.2	98.7	97.9	97.4	93.5	98.4	97.2	97.5	98.1
Materials	50	55.0	57.7	57.3	58.5	57.9	54.5	57.8	58.2	58.1	58.0
Employment costs	25	25.2	22.9	23.2	22.5	22.6	22.3	22.2	22.1	21.5	22.1
Industrial services	4	4.8	4.5	4.3	3.9	3.4	3.1	3.0	3.1	3.1	3.1
Other services	9	8.2	8.2	8.5	7.3	7.6	7.6	9.3	8.6	8.5	8.6
Interest payments	2	1.4	2.0	1.7	1.3	1.8	2.1	2.2	1.9	2.3	2.3
Taxes	4	4.2	4.0	3.7	4.4	4.1	3.9	3.9	3.3	4.0	4.0
Disposable funds	6	1.2	0.8	1.3	2.1	2.6	6.5	1.6	2.8	2.5	1.9
Other funds	4	3.4	3.3	3.4	3.5	4.1	4.3	4.6	4.5	4.0	3.9
Available funds	10	4.6	4.1	4.8	5.6	6.7	10.8	6.2	7.3	6.5	5.8
For investment	6	5.3	4.8	4.4	4.2	4.4	4.6	4.6	4.2	5.2	4.7
R&D and innovation	2	0.7	0.7	0.7	0.6	0.7	0.7	0.8	0.8	1.1	0.8
Fixed capital	4	4.6	4.1	3.7	3.5	3.7	3.9	3.8	3.4	4.1	4.0
Surplus/deficit	4	-0.7	-0.7	0.3	1.5	2.3	6.2	1.6	3.1	1.2	1.1

Table 49   Wholesale price indices for textiles in Japan compared with consumer price index (1980 = 100)

	Wholesale price indices (Yen basis)			
	Import prices	Export prices	Domestic prices	Consumer price index
1970	53.5	76.4	62.0	423.
1971	53.9	73.6	60.0	44.8
1972	57.4	69.8	62.0	46.9
1973	90.8	86.2	84.5	52.4
1974	88.7	95.8	83.9	65.2
1975	78.2	89.1	81.3	72.9
1976	94.6	92.3	90.4	79.7
1977	87.9	83.4	89.1	86.1
1978	76.2	80.6	91.8	89.4
1979	86.7	89.1	95.2	92.6
1980	100.0	100.0	100.0	100.0
1981	98.0	99.3	101.0	104.9
1982	101.4	97.9	102.9	107.7
1983	99.1	93.0	101.1	109.7
1984	100.4	92.5	103.4	112.1
1985	93.8	91.9	102.2	114.4
1986	76.5	81.4	94.6	114.9
1987	76.8	83.4	94.1	114.7

Source: Research and Statistical Department, Bank of Japan, *Economic Statistics Annual*, 1986

Table 50 Pattern of costs in the textile industry in Japan: as a percentage of the value of sales

	Norm	1972	1974	1975	1977	1980	1981	1982	1983	1984	1985
For current output	94	95.6	98.8	99.2	98.6	96.6	96.2	96.3	96.7	95.3	97.3
Materials	50	55.0	56.6	55.7	56.4	55.2	55.1	55.2	54.5	54.1	54.2
Employment costs	25	17.5	18.7	19.2	19.1	18.1	18.4	18.7	19.1	19.0	19.9
Industrial services	4	7.3	6.9	7.1	6.9	7.1	7.6	7.6	7.6	7.6	7.6
Other services	9	10.4	10.2	11.0	10.6	11.0	9.7	9.6	10.6	9.4	11.0
Interest payments	2	3.7	4.6	4.9	4.2	3.7	3.8	3.6	3.5	3.4	3.0
Taxes	4	1.7	1.7	1.3	1.4	1.5	1.5	1.6	1.5	1.6	1.7
Disposable funds	6	4.4	1.2	0.8	1.4	3.4	3.8	3.7	3.3	4.7	2.7
Other funds	4	3.4	3.5	3.2	3.2	2.4	2.6	2.6	2.6	2.5	2.1
Available funds	10	7.7	4.7	4.0	4.6	5.8	6.4	6.3	5.9	7.2	4.8
For investment	6	5.2	4.8	3.8	3.2	3.6	4.4	4.4	4.2	4.6	4.0
R&D and innovation	2	0.7	0.8	0.9	0.7	1.1	2.2	1.7	1.8	2.0	1.6
Fixed capital	4	4.4	4.0	2.8	2.5	2.5	2.2	2.8	2.4	2.6	2.3
Surplus/deficit	4	2.6	-0.2	0.2	1.4	2.2	2.0	1.9	1.7	2.6	0.8

Table 51 Investment expenditure in the textile industry: as a percentage of the value of sales

	1972	1975	1976	1977	1978	1979	1980	1981	1982	1983	1984	1985
United Kingdom												
Total investment	4.7	4.9	4.1	4.0	4.8	4.9	4.6	4.1	4.4	4.5	5.1	5.3
R&D	0.1	0.1	0.1	0.1	0.1	0.1	0.1	0.1	0.2	0.2	0.2	0.2
Innovation	0.5	0.6	0.4	0.4	0.4	0.4	0.5	0.5	0.5	0.7	0.7	0.7
Fixed capital	4.1	4.3	3.5	3.5	4.3	4.3	3.9	3.4	3.7	3.7	4.2	4.5
West Germany												
Total investment	5.9	4.9	5.3	5.3	5.2	6.0	5.8	5.1	5.3	6.3	6.0	6.4
R&D	0.3	0.2	0.2	0.2	0.2	0.3	0.2	0.2	0.3	0.3	0.3	0.3
Innovation	0.6	0.6	0.6	0.6	0.7	0.8	0.7	0.8	0.8	0.9	0.8	0.8
Fixed capital	5.0	4.2	4.5	4.5	4.4	5.0	4.9	4.1	4.3	5.2	4.9	5.3
United States												
Total investment	5.3	4.4	4.2	4.2	4.4	4.1	4.4	4.6	4.6	4.2	5.2	4.7
R&D	0.2	0.2	0.2	0.1	0.2	0.2	0.2	0.2	0.2	0.2	0.3	0.3
Innovation	0.5	0.5	0.5	0.5	0.5	0.5	0.6	0.6	0.6	0.6	0.8	0.5
Fixed capital	4.6	3.7	3.5	3.5	3.7	3.4	3.7	3.9	3.8	3.4	4.1	4.0
Japan												
Total investment	5.2	3.8	3.4	3.2	2.9	3.7	3.6	4.4	4.4	4.2	4.6	4.0
R&D	0.2	0.3	0.2	0.2	0.2	0.3	0.3	0.6	0.5	0.5	0.5	0.8
Innovation	0.5	0.7	0.5	0.5	0.6	0.9	0.8	1.6	1.2	1.2	1.5	0.8
Fixed capital	4.4	2.8	2.6	2.5	2.0	2.5	2.5	2.2	2.8	2.4	2.6	2.3

Figure 22 Textiles: total investment expenditure

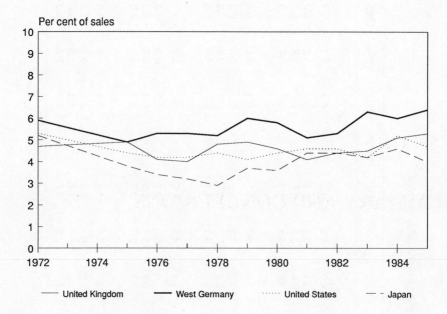

PART III

SUMMARY AND CONCLUSIONS

14 Country summaries

There are different ways of summarising the information collected for these twenty industries. But in so far as we have concentrated on the industries in the previous chapters it is useful now to turn our attention to each country – comparing the output performance in each of their five industries (Table 52, p.119 and Figures 23 to 26, pp.121-122).

United Kingdom
In view of the belief in the decline of British manufacturing, it is interesting to note that from 1948 to 1973 the index of the volume of output for these industries recorded a steady rise. British manufacturing companies developed the new technologies and increased output, but not so fast as their international competitors.

Figure 24 shows that the four traditional industries increased output up to 1973 – but thereafter output of three fell. The output of chemicals continued the rising trend, reacted to the troubles of 1971 and 1979, but then joined in the general recovery. It has been suggested earlier that the removal of the price and other restrictions on competition by the Competition Act 1980 made possible the general recovery from 1981 to 1987. The turning point is even clearer when the index is based on 1980.

West Germany
The indices of output demonstrate the steady if undramatic progress made by the four traditional industries in West Germany for which we have full information (Figure 24). Apart from the recessions of 1967 and 1973 the growth of output in all four has been continuous; only textiles have, on occasion, shown a reduced output. It can be argued, therefore, that the emphasis on product quality, with its associated high R&D expenditure, government-assisted technology transfer and co-operation from the unions has provided the economic and cultural basis for competitiveness of a high order. Furthermore German manufacturers do not suffer the disturbance caused by actual or threatened takeovers. Nicholaus-Jürgen Weikart, a Frankfurt corporate lawyer, summarised the situation[1]:

> The German system is, simply, not designed to maximise shareholder wealth but rather to ensure the well-being of management, workers and shareholders.

This situation shows every sign of continuing. The Deutsche Bundesbank commented in its report for June 1988[2]:

> In the first few months of 1988 economic developments in the Federal Republic of Germany were marked by vigorous growth and by still relatively stable prices.

Growth of output was accompanied by a profound improvement in business sentiment, after the turmoil in the share and foreign exchange markets had temporarily led to uncertainty towards the end of last year.

United States

The pattern of industrial growth in the United States is more complicated (Figure 25, p.122). Despite problems at the time of the first oil shock, output increased until 1979. The change in trend after 1979 suggests that – while the second oil price shock added to the difficulties – the main problem was competition from Japan. This situation has been attributed to complacency among American producers, 'America's manufacturing myopia'[3] as it has been described. Judging by a survey of United States firms commissioned by the consultants Cooper & Lybrand, many American manufacturing executives still view other United States companies as their primary competition and are confident about the United States' ability to remain competitive globally. The myopia focuses on competition across the street, rather than on the greater threat from across the ocean. Lessons that should have been learned from the various problems affecting cars, steel and machine tools, have been lost on other manufacturing segments. But it is equally true that from 1982 there is clear evidence that the companies in the four traditional industries studied here had learned their lesson, were fighting back and regaining ground. The output indices show a distinct upturn and the increases in R&D expenditure, particularly in motor vehicles, suggest that far more attention is being paid to product development.

Japan

The growth of Japanese industry is much as would be expected; only the textile industry has failed to grow (Figure 26, p.122).

But as has been described, the rapid growth has been made at the cost of some potential financial instability. Market share has been gained, but prices have been low relative to costs – low enough to attract the charges of dumping. Only history can show whether high output, at any price, is a viable economic procedure in the long-term.

15 Implications for policy

The research suggests a number of ideas for policy consideration across the range of countries studied. They fall under six main headings.

Research and innovation

The key to sustained growth and financial viability is an adequate input of intangible investment, measured as expenditure on R&D, innovation and licences. Thus any industry that falls behind the going rate for its particular technology is courting trouble, and industrial policy requires that this vital area of cash flow be monitored annually. The funding of the commercialisation of new scientific and market ideas (innovation) must be measured in parallel with that of the generally less important expenditure on fixed assets.

Research and innovation is normally carried on within the company but it may be sub-contracted. However, as was seen in Japan, collaborative research, within enterprise groups or with the sponsorship of government laboratories, is a viable alternative for part of the effort. Consortia and collaborative research should be explored in more detail. Small and medium-sized companies are very dependent on this type of government sponsorship, and large ones, even the 950 companies that fund R&D in Britain, can benefit by pooling their resources in new, risky areas, when technologies are promising but largely undeveloped.

Accounting practices

Accounting conventions should be widened so that all expenditure on research and innovation is accounted for and reported so that it is fully monitored by the boards of companies. These disbursements must be seen as the parallel streams of cash that ensure the future of the company – not as profits foregone or as an unacceptable overhead. Expenditure on fixed assets (or tangible investment) is an associated expenditure not important in its own right, but undertaken to underpin essential product and process development and, as necessary, the expansion of output.

The service revolution

The structure of employment in manufacturing industry has changed and there is some evidence that this has weakened rather than strengthened companies. Further research is required to test whether the growing dependence on outside expertise is wise or, alternatively, has led to loss of corporate morale and to excessive costs.

Government involvement
The analysis of the varied experience of the four countries has shown that, in the modern world, government must be involved in industry, taking a supportive role. But because their knowledge will always be insufficient, civil servants should not be directly involved in detailed manipulation of company structure. However, removing obstacles to growth and sustaining a comprehensive technological infrastructure (especially for small firms) have proved immensely valuable and should be encouraged.

Best practice
Taking all factors into consideration, the best practice would seem to be found in West Germany. Manufacturers, with encouragement from the Federal Government, aim to produce high quality, specialty products for which they obtain high prices. The higher margins obtained are spent within the company as tangible and intangible investment. It follows that output rises steadily from a sound financial base. The Japanese achievement is more spectacular, even more technologically brilliant; but the technique of obtaining market share by discounting prices has left some companies in Japanese industries heavily in debt and very vulnerable. Their practice is to be studied rather than copied.

Defining success
A still unsolved problem lies in the definition of success. Do policy makers judge this according to the level of output? By market share? Or according to financial stability? Is success seen as short-term or must it ensure long-term growth? Can a high market share associated with financial vulnerability be accounted as success? The answers to these questions must remain a matter of judgement but judgement taken in the light of the history of the original economic base and of the industrial policy of each country.

16 The lessons for Britain

This study, by assembling the data on manufacturing revenue and costs for a historical analysis, has taken a first step in explaining the differences in competitiveness that have been observed over three decades, especially between Britain and its competitors.

There is no real mystery. In four of the five industries the British ones have had fewer resources available for innovation than their competitors. If there is one dominant explanation of this it is that industrial economists and planners in both industry and government have not until very recently followed industrial scientists and technologists into the technological age. They have concentrated on the current manufacturing operation (thus the preoccupation with 'productivity') when equal emphasis should have been on the future and on ways of providing products to meet future world demand. When around 20 per cent of the sales revenue of an electronics company has to be devoted to the technological needs of the future and to market intelligence, it is almost beyond belief that this fact is not apparent in company balance sheets, nor incorporated in the calculations of statisticians and econometricians.

The loss of competitiveness happened because there was a profound lack of understanding, in the country and in the civil service and even in some companies, of the role of industrial technology – and what it costs to remain competitive. The awakening of the positive culture that grew out of the war-time successes, the technological universities and the pioneer work of the Ministry of Technology, was counteracted by the stronger influence of those in authority who failed to understand, who saw industrial science as peripheral or a free good, and to whom a science ministry was an anathema. Furthermore, price control offset much of the help given to companies under the Industry Act of 1972.

The forces that determine the essential company expenditure on research and innovation are a function of the technology and the speed at which it is being introduced by competitive companies – and both can be, and are, influenced by government procurement and pressures. If British industry is to complete its recovery and maintain a rising trend, it needs help with technological transfer equivalent to that available under the Ministry of Technology between 1964 and 1970. The Japanese Government is currently building and financing seven new collaborative research laboratories directed to the emerging technologies; these adding to the 16 MITI institutes already working for manufacturing industry. In Britain, however, the government maintains its policy of reducing funding for long-term research. This is a matter that needs the immediate attention of government ministers.

References to Part III

1. Quoted in D. Goodhart, 'The corporate poison pill', *Financial Times*, 12 August 1988.
2. *Monthly report of the Deutsche Bundesbank*, Vol. 40, No. 6, p. 5.
3. *Strategic Direction*, Strategic Direction Publishers Ltd., Zürich, Switzerland, 1988.

Tables and figures to Part III

Table 52   Index of output (1970 = 100)

	United Kingdom					West Germany				
	Mechanical engineering	Motor vehicles	Chemicals	Textiles	All manu-facturing	Mechanical engineering	Motor vehicles	Chemicals	Textiles	All manu-facturing
1960	66.6	72.4	55.6	80.7	74.7	66.2	48.4	37.0	71.8	58.0
1961	72.1	65.2	56.4	77.9	74.9	72.6	50.6	39.3	73.5	61.0
1962	71.7	69.3	58.7	76.5	75.0	73.5	55.0	43.0	76.3	63.7
1963	71.6	80.7	63.0	80.3	77.7	71.3	61.1	47.2	79.1	65.6
1964	78.3	90.0	69.3	85.2	84.7	76.5	65.4	53.3	80.2	72.0
1965	82.8	90.6	74.1	87.6	87.1	81.6	68.7	58.5	84.0	75.8
1966	88.0	89.4	78.2	87.4	88.8	80.9	70.3	64.1	84.0	77.1
1967	88.4	84.7	82.8	85.6	89.3	75.0	60.0	69.7	77.9	75.2
1968	92.8	94.4	89.9	98.6	96.0	79.4	74.2	81.3	90.1	83.4
1969	97.7	99.1	94.8	101.5	99.6	92.6	90.1	93.3	99.2	94.3
1970	100.0	100.0	100.0	100.0	100.0	100.0	100.0	100.0	100.0	100.0
1971	94.8	97.5	101.9	99.2	98.9	100.0	100.6	106.2	105.3	102.5
1972	90.1	99.6	107.7	100.7	101.1	96.3	100.6	113.1	109.2	106.4
1973	99.4	104.2	120.4	105.4	110.4	101.9	108.3	126.8	108.1	112.6
1974	105.8	96.1	127.0	96.4	109.1	102.6	97.5	130.2	101.8	109.9
1975	103.9	87.1	113.6	88.7	96.8	96.0	101.9	114.2	98.6	103.2
1976	99.8	88.0	128.4	91.5	103.4	99.3	115.8	132.3	108.6	111.9
1977	99.2	94.9	132.7	92.3	105.4	101.0	122.3	132.1	106.1	114.4
1978	96.7	89.8	134.2	89.1	106.1	103.3	123.2	138.0	102.3	116.2
1979	93.4	87.5	138.1	85.4	105.9	109.0	130.0	145.8	104.7	122.5
1980	85.8	75.6	124.9	70.6	96.7	113.5	124.6	141.8	103.5	122.5
1981	76.5	62.8	124.9	64.8	90.9	110.7	128.4	142.0	97.0	119.3
1982	77.6	60.6	125.8	63.3	91.1	109.5	128.4	137.4	91.8	115.6
1983	74.6	63.5	135.1	64.7	93.7	107.8	133.3	147.0	92.5	116.7
1984	76.4	62.4	151.1	66.4	97.5	112.8	132.6	156.8	95.4	121.1
1985	79.6	65.1	148.2	69.1	100.3	123.3	149.1	160.9	98.8	126.2
1986	76.8	63.8	151.0	69.3	101.2	128.9	154.9	160.2	99.0	128.8
1987	77.5	69.1	161.5	72.1	107.1	127.0	157.7	164.3	97.2	129.5

continued...

Source: United Kingdom: Historical series of the index of industrial production. Economic Trends, *British Business*
West Germany: VDMA *Statistisches Handbuch für den Machinenbau*

Table 52 (cont'd)

	United States					Japan				
	Machinery*	Motor vehicles	Chemicals	Textiles	All manu-facturing	Mechanical engineering	Motor vehicles	Chemicals	Textiles	All manu-facturing
1960	54.5	80.9	46.8	62.0	64.3	21.0	9.1	25.7	45.5	27.4
1961	53.1	71.0	49.2	63.9	62.5	25.7	15.4	29.3	49.1	32.9
1962	59.5	86.5	54.6	68.2	67.2	29.6	18.7	33.6	51.0	35.7
1963	63.5	95.7	59.6	70.6	71.2	33.2	24.3	37.2	55.7	39.8
1964	72.4	98.3	65.4	76.2	76.1	37.9	32.2	42.2	61.6	46.3
1965	81.4	125.6	72.9	83.0	84.3	36.4	35.5	46.2	65.9	48.1
1966	94.6	123.4	79.4	88.0	92.0	40.3	43.2	51.7	72.6	54.5
1967	95.8	108.3	83.1	89.4	94.0	53.5	59.5	61.0	79.2	65.3
1968	97.5	130.3	90.9	96.5	100.0	70.5	77.3	72.5	84.0	75.5
1969	104.7	126.2	98.3	100.7	104.3	83.5	88.4	85.7	92.2	87.8
1970	100.0	100.0	100.0	100.0	100.0	100.0	100.0	100.0	100.0	100.0
1971	96.0	128.5	104.6	104.2	101.7	96.5	109.9	106.8	104.0	102.7
1972	111.1	147.1	120.2	120.2	111.7	97.3	119.0	116.2	105.3	110.3
1973	128.1	161.2	128.3	127.8	122.0	119.2	133.9	132.0	114.1	129.8
1974	134.2	138.9	132.4	118.8	121.6	118.2	123.9	128.5	99.8	126.7
1975	119.8	120.4	122.3	109.4	109.3	98.2	131.2	116.2	94.0	110.7
1976	128.8	153.8	141.9	120.4	122.5	115.4	148.3	130.2	102.7	120.6
1977	137.5	174.5	154.2	120.2	130.1	122.7	161.0	136.1	101.1	125.6
1978	147.1	184.1	164.0	123.0	138.0	134.8	175.3	152.8	102.5	133.7
1979	156.8	173.2	175.9	129.7	144.4	137.7	182.2	168.9	104.1	143.6
1980	155.9	128.9	172.0	124.0	137.9	150.2	208.8	162.4	102.7	150.4
1981	164.0	132.5	179.1	121.4	141.3	153.5	211.4	159.2	101.1	151.9
1982	142.7	119.0	162.9	111.4	129.3	151.1	202.9	160.7	99.9	152.5
1983	144.3	148.5	178.6	125.9	139.3	149.9	210.1	169.8	99.4	157.7
1984	173.2	182.8	190.7	129.4	156.0	169.1	216.8	184.7	101.7	174.4
1985	177.2	193.0	199.1	128.8	159.8	181.8	232.0	189.7	101.0	183.5
1986	173.1	191.9	208.4	141.2	163.2	184.7	231.8	190.9	96.9	183.0
1987	182.3	192.4	221.3	149.9	170.3	193.3	231.6	205.0	95.6	190.3

Source: USA: *Business Statistics*, Supplement to Survey of Current Business; Japan: *Economic Statistics Annual*, The Bank of Japan
* Includes office and computing machines

Figure 23 United Kingdom industries: index of output (1970 = 100)

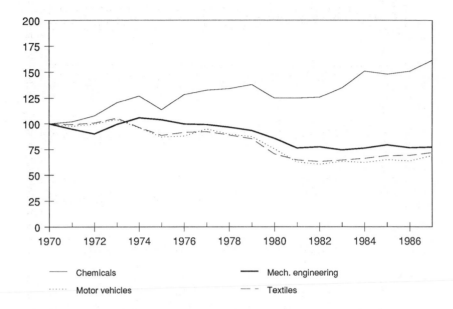

— Chemicals   — Mech. engineering

⋯⋯ Motor vehicles   − − Textiles

Figure 24 West German industries: index of output (1970 = 100)

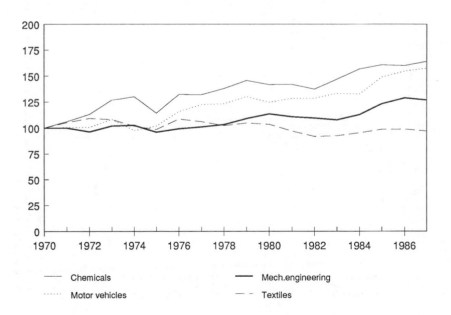

— Chemicals   — Mech.engineering

⋯⋯ Motor vehicles   − − Textiles

Figure 25   United States industries: index of output (1970 = 100)

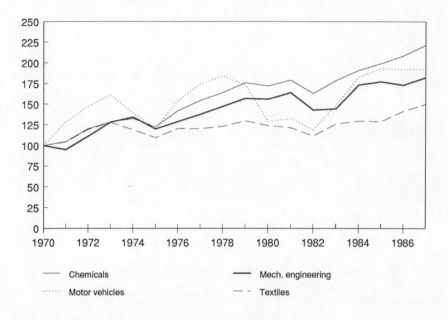

- —— Chemicals
- ·········· Motor vehicles
- —— Mech. engineering
- – – Textiles

Figure 26   Japanese industries: index of output (1970 = 100)

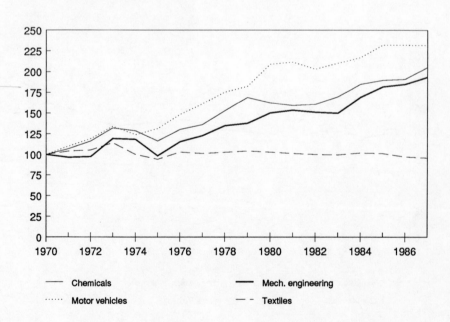

- —— Chemicals
- ·········· Motor vehicles
- —— Mech. engineering
- – – Textiles

Appendix A

International comparisons 1972 to 1986

A1   Market share of OECD exports

A2   Import penetration

Table A1 Market share of OECD exports

	1972	1973	1974	1975	1976	1977	1978	1979	1980	1981	1982	1983	1984	1985	1986
Mechanical engineering															
United Kingdom	10.7	9.2	8.7	9.4	8.8	9.3	9.0	9.1	9.9	8.6	8.7	7.8	7.5	7.5	7.2
West Germany	25.4	27.4	26.3	23.3	24.2	24.4	23.6	23.3	21.3	19.2	20.2	20.7	19.9	20.9	24.1
USA	20.4	19.7	21.2	22.9	22.8	20.2	18.9	19.3	20.2	23.3	22.8	19.6	19.6	18.4	14.1
Japan	6.7	7.1	7.9	7.4	8.1	9.3	10.8	9.9	10.3	13.3	12.6	14.5	15.9	15.9	15.8
Electronics															
United Kingdom	7.6	7.3	7.5	8.4	7.2	7.6	7.6	8.0	7.9	6.5	6.9	6.6	6.7	7.5	7.0
West Germany	16.6	17.3	17.1	16.3	15.6	15.2	15.1	14.9	13.9	12.0	11.9	11.0	9.7	10.4	12.0
USA	21.4	21.7	23.4	21.9	21.2	21.5	20.4	21.4	22.3	23.7	26.3	25.6	25.2	23.4	20.7
Japan	22.5	22.2	20.0	19.4	25.2	24.5	25.7	23.8	25.5	30.9	28.5	31.6	34.6	33.1	34.2
Motor vehicles															
United Kingdom	8.2	7.5	7.2	7.6	6.6	6.5	6.4	6.2	6.3	5.3	4.8	3.9	3.4	3.5	3.3
West Germany	21.6	23.9	22.1	20.6	21.3	21.6	21.4	22.7	22.1	20.8	23.2	21.2	19.0	19.3	22.2
USA	16.3	16.1	17.6	18.7	17.1	15.4	14.3	14.0	12.4	13.7	12.1	12.1	13.3	13.3	10.5
Japan	13.7	12.8	15.9	14.4	16.4	18.4	20.2	18.9	23.2	26.5	24.7	25.7	26.8	27.6	28.9
Chemicals															
United Kingdom	9.4	8.7	8.8	9.0	8.9	9.7	9.5	9.4	9.7	9.0	9.5	9.0	8.9	9.6	9.6
West Germany	20.5	21.8	21.0	19.4	20.3	20.1	20.1	20.3	19.2	18.4	18.7	19.0	18.7	18.9	20.7
USA	17.1	17.0	16.5	17.3	17.3	16.6	16.7	17.4	18.5	20.0	18.3	17.5	18.5	16.3	14.6
Japan	8.2	7.3	8.5	8.6	7.4	7.5	6.9	6.2	6.3	6.7	6.6	7.1	7.1	7.1	7.4
Textiles															
United Kingdom	8.9	8.8	8.6	8.2	8.0	8.5	8.3	8.6	8.4	6.8	6.5	6.2	6.1	6.5	6.1
West Germany	15.1	16.9	16.6	15.8	16.6	15.9	16.2	17.0	15.6	14.7	15.6	15.6	15.7	16.3	18.2
USA	6.1	7.1	8.6	8.0	8.6	7.6	7.6	5.6	9.3	9.7	8.2	7.1	6.9	6.0	6.0
Japan	16.2	13.5	14.3	14.2	14.2	14.3	12.6	11.3	12.6	15.4	14.4	15.4	14.9	13.3	12.2

Source: OECD, Directorate for Science, Technology and Industry

Table A2   Import penetration

	1972	1973	1974	1975	1976	1977	1978	1979	1980	1981	1982	1983	1984	1985
Mechanical engineering														
United Kingdom	18.3	23.9	27.2	25.4	29.6	30.6	29.7	30.1	29.4	30.0	32.8	35.7	38.9	41.1
West Germany	21.7	22.0	23.4	26.2	29.3	28.3	28.3	28.4	28.9	31.0	31.2	31.8	37.4	40.0
USA	5.3	5.5	6.0	6.7	6.7	6.7	8.1	8.6	9.1	9.5	10.2	10.5	12.7	13.0
Japan	3.2	3.7	4.4	4.4	3.8	3.5	3.2	3.9	4.1	3.5	4.0	3.6	3.8	3.9
Electronics														
United Kingdom	22.3	31.6	33.4	32.8	37.6	40.6	41.3	42.3	35.5	45.1	51.6	55.3	58.7	59.9
West Germany	27.4	31.0	32.9	36.6	41.0	39.7	42.1	46.1	50.6	57.5	61.9	64.8	69.5	86.3
USA	10.7	12.1	13.2	12.6	16.0	14.7	15.6	14.6	14.2	15.2	14.9	17.4	21.8	23.2
Japan	4.4	4.8	6.3	6.1	5.8	5.5	4.6	5.7	5.7	4.8	4.9	4.2	4.4	5.8
Motor vehicles														
United Kingdom	17.6	20.3	20.3	25.5	28.8	34.8	36.4	41.9	40.8	43.9	49.0	53.3	51.0	51.3
West Germany	22.8	22.8	24.1	25.3	26.6	26.8	27.9	26.9	27.0	28.9	31.9	32.2	35.9	34.4
USA	12.3	12.2	15.4	15.1	14.1	13.6	15.8	16.8	21.8	21.2	22.8	20.7	21.8	28.3
Japan	0.7	0.9	1.2	1.3	1.1	1.1	1.0	1.3	1.1	0.8	0.9	1.0	1.1	1.1
Chemicals														
United Kingdom	14.9	17.3	21.4	18.7	20.4	22.2	24.9	25.3	25.5	28.2	31.0	33.7	36.0	37.3
West Germany	18.6	20.2	23.3	22.5	24.3	25.1	27.1	30.1	30.8	33.1	34.5	35.2	38.7	41.9
USA	4.1	4.4	5.5	4.8	5.3	5.3	6.5	6.7	7.2	7.0	7.2	7.5	8.8	7.8
Japan	6.2	7.3	8.6	6.6	7.4	7.0	6.7	8.1	8.3	8.4	9.4	9.2	10.0	9.4
Textiles														
United Kingdom	16.2	18.5	21.4	19.9	22.2	23.2	26.7	28.5	29.7	33.3	34.9	38.0	40.2	42.0
West Germany	24.7	27.1	27.4	28.1	30.4	31.8	34.0	36.6	37.6	39.4	40.0	41.4	43.9	45.7
USA	4.9	4.7	4.6	3.7	4.2	4.0	4.9	4.6	4.9	5.5	5.3	5.4	7.0	7.3
Japan	5.4	8.3	7.7	6.1	6.3	5.9	7.2	8.7	7.6	7.5	8.5	7.3	9.1	8.2

Source: OECD, Directorate for Science, Technology and Industry

Computer analysis of the flow of funds in the mechanical engineering industry in West Germany in 1984

B1 Investment and flow of funds

B2 Analysis of manpower costs, employment and import peneration

Table B1   Investment and flow of funds

	Expenditure (million DM)			As a percentage of:		
	For all uses	Current output	R&D/ innov.	Value of sales %	Value added %	
Total current	129977	119518	10460	89.70		
Materials	58005	56409	1596	42.33		
Employment costs	48001	41484	6517	31.13	68.17	
wages/salaries	39481	34121		25.61	56.07	
social costs	8520	7363		5.53	12.10	
Industrial services	4791	4791		3.60		
Other services	13535	11187	2347	8.40		
Interest payments	2425	2425		1.82	3.98	
Indirect taxes	1422	1422		1.07	2.34	
Direct taxes	1799	1799		1.35	2.96	
Total investment			16911	12.69	27.79	100.00
R&D			3828	2.87	6.29	22.64
Innovation *			6428	4.82	10.56	38.01
Licences			920	0.69	1.51	5.44
Fixed capital	6451	716	5735	4.30	9.42	33.91
Total sales	133246					100.00
Home sales	63909					47.96
Exports	69337					52.04
Derived variables						
Gross earnings		76837		57.67		
Value added		60858		45.67	100.00	
Disposable funds		13728		10.30	22.56	
Other funds		9764		7.33	16.04	
Available funds		23492		17.63	38.60	
Deduct investment		16911		12.69	27.79	
Surplus/deficit		6581		4.94	10.81	
Distribution						
Total		6581		4.94	10.81	100.00
To working proprietors		193		0.14	0.32	2.92
To shareholders		1066		0.80	1.75	16.20
For investment overseas		338		0.25	0.56	5.14
Working capital/reserves		4985		3.74	8.19	75.74
Detail of other funds						
Total		9764		7.33	16.04	100.00
Merchanting		1920		1.44	3.15	19.66
Plant sales		2248		1.69	3.69	23.02
Other receipts		5596		4.20	9.20	57.32
of which:						
Investment income		1399		1.05	2.30	14.33
Foreign investment		338		0.25	0.56	3.46
Production subsidies		76		0.06	0.12	0.78

Table B2   Analysis of manpower costs, employment and import penetration

	Manpower costs Million DM		Unit costs DM	Number employed
Total employees	48001		51543	931278
Current output employees	41484		49746	833919
Investment employees				
Total	6517		66936	97359
R&D	2384		68758	34675
Innovation *	4133		65927	62684
Analysis of industry manpower				
Salaried employees	22789		65927	345673
Operatives	25211		43052	585605
Working proprietors and				
family workers	193		66587	2891
Summary of manpower data				
Investment employees and costs				
as a percentage of:		%		
All employees		10.45		
All employment costs		13.58		
Salaried employees		28.17		
Salary costs		28.60		
Import penetration				
Imports			19540	
Sales plus imports minus exports (demand)			83449	
			%	
Imports as a percentage of demand			23.42	

* Design, product development, market intelligence, planning, industrial engineering, tooling, manufacturing start-up

Source: Statistisches Bundesamt, *Kostenstruktur der Unternehmen im Investitionsgüter produzierenden Gewerbe* (Reihe 4.3.2), *Beschäftigte, Umsatz und Investitionen der Unternehmen und Betriebe* (4.2.1), *Preise und Preisindizes für gewerbliche Produkte (Erzeugerpreise)* – Facherie 17; Deutsche Bundesbank, *Monthly Report*, November and May; VDMA; Stifterverband für die Deutsche Wissenschaft, *Forschung und Entwicklung in der Wirtschaft, 1972 to 1985*

Appendix C

Patterns of costs 1972 to 1985, industry by country

The analysis of cost patterns discussed at the beginning of the report is explained and illustrated diagrammatically here. For example, in Figure C1 (p.130)covering all manufacturing industry in the United Kingdom, the total value of sales is equal to 100. The left-hand column of the diagram represents the gross receipts from sales. The upper part shows the value of purchases of materials, components and fuel needed for production, the remainder is the value of the 'margin added to materials' or 'gross earnings'.

The margin added is carried to the second column and comprises the remaining costs associated with production and sales and a residual. These costs are:

- payment for industrial and other services provided by people outside the organisation
- employment costs (wages, salaries and social costs) of those employed on line operations (the 'employment budget')
- interest payments
- direct and indirect taxes.

The residual, when these costs are met, represents the 'disposable funds', and these are carried into the third column. This, in turn, divides into the expenditure on tangible and intangible investment and the distribution to working proprietors, board members, the providers of capital, etc. As will be shown later, disposable funds are augmented by income from factoring, sale of fixed assets, interest from investments, new equity, subsidies, etc. Such 'below the line' receipts add from 5-10 per cent to sales receipts.

The value added is shown in the second column of the cash flow model, being the gross earnings less the payments made by the industry for outside services. Value added is seen as the contribution made by those employed in the industry.

By way of further illustration, Figures C2 to C5 (pp.131-134) show the cost structures for the chemical industries in the four countries of the study. These diagrams for the chemical industry represent the data given in statistical form in Tables C13 to C16 (pp.147-150)

The other tables in this appendix refer to mechanical engineering (Tables C1-C4, pp.135-138), electronics (Tables C5-C8, pp.139-142), motor vehicles (Tables C9-C12, pp.143-146) and textiles (Tables C17-C20, pp.151-154).

Figure C1   Pattern of costs in all manufacturing in the United Kingdom in 1984

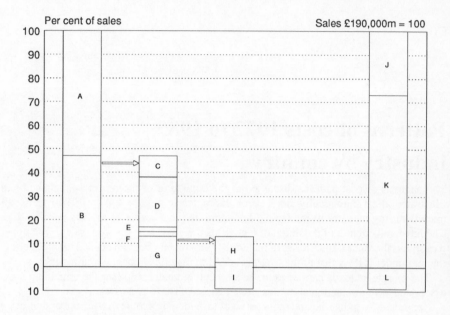

Key

A = Purchase of materials for production
B = Gross earnings

H = Tangible and intangible investment
I = Surplus for reserves, working proprietors board members and providers of capital

C = Professional and industrial services
D = Employment costs
E = Interest payments
F = Direct and indirect taxes
G = Disposable funds

J = Export sales
K = Home sales
L = Other funds (sale of fixed assets, interest receipts, equity, foreign investment, subsidies etc)

Figure C2   Pattern of costs in the chemical industry in the United Kingdom in 1984

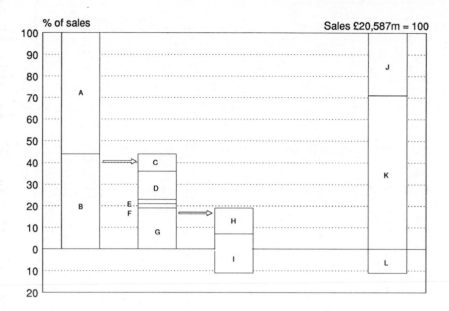

Key

A = Purchase of materials for production

B = Gross earnings

H = Tangible and intangible investment

I = Surplus for reserves, working proprietors board members and providers of capital

C = Professional and industrial services

D = Employment costs

E = Interest payments

F = Direct and indirect taxes

G = Disposable funds

J = Export sales

K = Home sales

L = Other funds (sale of fixed assets, interest receipts, equity, foreign investment, subsidies etc)

Figure C3   Pattern of costs in the chemical industry in West Germany in 1984

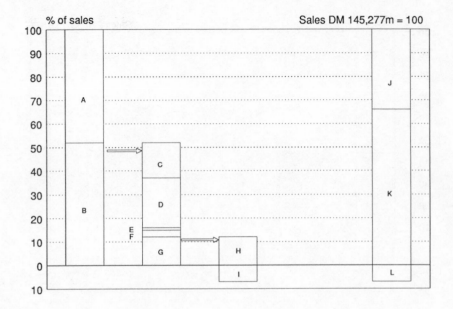

Key

A = Purchase of materials for production

B = Gross earnings

C = Professional and industrial services

D = Employment costs

E = Interest payments

F = Direct and indirect taxes

G = Disposable funds

H = Tangible and intangible investment

I = Surplus for reserves, working proprietors board members and providers of capital

J = Export sales

K = Home sales

L = Other funds (sale of fixed assets, interest receipts, equity, foreign investment, subsidies etc)

Figure C4   Pattern of costs in the chemical industry in the United States in 1984

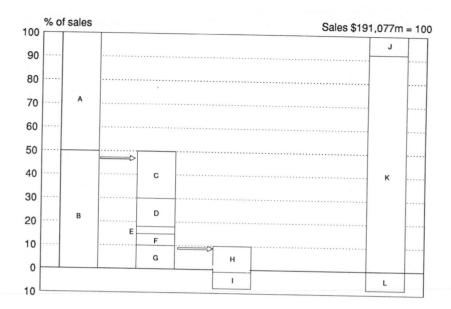

Key

A = Purchase of materials for production
B = Gross earnings

H = Tangible and intangible investment
I = Surplus for reserves, working
    proprietors board members and
    providers of capital

C = Professional and industrial services
D = Employment costs
E = Interest payments
F = Direct and indirect taxes
G = Disposable funds

J = Export sales
K = Home sales
L = Other funds (sale of fixed assets,
    interest receipts, equity, foreign
    investment, subsidies etc)

Figure C5 Pattern of costs in the chemical industry in Japan in 1984

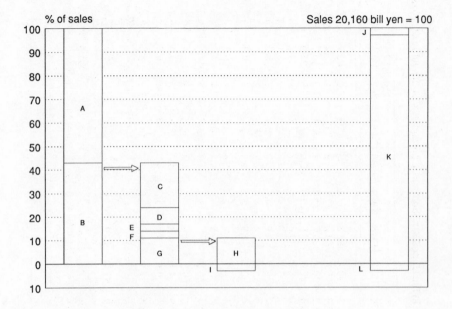

Key

A = Purchase of materials for production

B = Gross earnings

C = Professional and industrial services

D = Employment costs

E = Interest payments

F = Direct and indirect taxes

G = Disposable funds

H = Tangible and intangible investment

I = Surplus for reserves, working proprietors board members and providers of capital

J = Export sales

K = Home sales

L = Other funds (sale of fixed assets, interest receipts, equity, foreign investment, subsidies etc)

Table C1 Pattern of costs in the mechanical engineering industry in the United Kingdom: as a percentage of the value of sales

	Norm	1968	1972	1973	1974	1975	1976	1977	1978	1979	1980	1981	1982	1983	1984	1985
For current output	86	87.3	87.9	91.6	96.5	89.4	89.9	90.2	88.8	87.3	87.5	85.5	87.6	89.7	87.8	87.7
Materials	40	44.1	43.8	47.1	50.7	44.8	44.6	45.4	44.2	43.6	42.9	39.6	41.1	43.4	43.0	44.1
Employment costs	32	30.3	32.0	32.0	32.4	31.7	32.1	30.7	30.7	31.0	32.7	32.1	31.3	30.7	30.1	28.5
wages & salaries		27.8	29.3	29.3	29.4	28.3	28.5	26.8	26.5	26.6	28.0	27.4	26.9	26.6	26.2	24.9
social costs		2.5	2.7	2.7	3.0	3.4	3.6	3.9	4.3	4.5	4.7	4.7	4.4	4.2	3.9	3.6
Industrial services	4	5.2	4.2	4.7	5.9	5.0	4.7	5.3	5.3	4.6	3.8	3.8	5.1	5.1	4.2	4.4
Other services	6	1.7	3.4	3.3	3.3	4.2	4.7	4.8	4.6	4.0	3.7	5.7	5.6	5.9	5.8	6.0
Interest payments	2	1.0	1.4	1.5	1.7	1.6	1.3	1.4	1.4	1.6	2.1	2.0	1.9	1.8	1.8	1.7
Taxes	2	5.0	3.2	2.9	2.5	2.1	2.5	2.6	2.5	2.5	2.2	2.3	2.7	2.8	3.0	3.0
Disposable funds	14	12.7	12.1	8.4	3.5	10.6	10.1	9.8	11.2	12.7	12.5	14.5	12.4	10.3	12.2	12.3
Other funds	4	3.6	3.3	2.9	2.4	5.4	6.4	5.9	6.5	4.7	4.1	6.7	4.4	4.4	6.6	6.0
Available funds	18	16.3	15.4	11.4	5.9	16.1	16.5	15.8	17.7	17.4	16.6	21.2	16.8	14.6	18.8	18.3
For investment	10	10.3	7.9	7.8	8.3	7.7	8.0	8.7	9.3	9.4	9.4	9.5	9.5	9.4	10.5	9.6
R&D and innovation	6	5.9	3.9	4.0	4.1	3.9	3.9	4.1	4.4	4.5	4.8	5.3	5.2	5.2	6.0	5.2
Fixed capital	4	4.3	3.9	3.8	4.2	3.8	4.1	4.6	4.9	4.9	4.6	4.2	4.3	4.2	4.5	4.4
Surplus/deficit	8	6.0	7.6	3.5	-2.4	8.4	8.4	7.1	8.5	8.0	7.2	11.7	7.3	5.3	8.3	8.7
Value added	50	49.0	48.6	44.8	40.1	46.0	46.0	44.5	45.9	47.9	49.5	50.9	48.3	45.6	47.0	45.6

Source: Department of Trade and Industry, Business Statistics Office, *Report on the Census of Production* (PA1002); *Company Finance* (MA3), *Overseas Transactions* (MA4), *Industrial Research and Development* (MO14), *British Business* - indices of output and prices; Board of Inland Revenue, *Inland Revenue Statistics* and special analyses

Table C2   Pattern of costs in the mechanical engineering industry in West Germany: as a percentage of the value of sales

	Norm	1972	1973	1974	1975	1976	1977	1978	1979	1980	1981	1982	1983	1984	1985
For current output	86	82.5	85.4	85.4	90.9	91.9	94.2	91.3	93.5	93.7	93.7	92.1	89.9	89.7	87.7
Materials	40	38.3	38.2	38.2	38.3	42.7	42.2	39.6	42.3	41.4	41.2	41.5	40.5	42.3	41.8
Employment costs	32	31.4	31.0	31.7	35.9	33.8	35.5	33.7	34.3	34.3	35.0	33.3	32.6	31.1	29.6
wages & salaries		26.4	26.0	26.6	29.8	28.0	29.6	28.2	28.7	28.6	29.2	27.6	26.9	25.6	24.4
social costs		5.0	5.0	5.1	6.1	5.8	5.9	5.5	5.6	5.7	5.8	5.6	5.7	5.5	5.2
Industrial services	4	3.3	3.6	3.4	3.6	3.2	3.6	5.3	3.9	4.1	4.1	4.0	3.8	3.6	4.0
Other services	6	5.0	8.0	7.1	8.5	8.2	8.2	8.2	8.4	9.1	9.0	8.6	8.7	8.4	8.1
Interest payments	2	2.1	2.6	3.0	2.4	1.5	1.7	1.6	1.7	2.2	2.4	2.7	2.0	1.8	1.7
Taxes	2	2.4	2.0	2.0	2.2	2.5	3.0	2.9	2.9	2.5	2.0	2.0	2.3	2.4	2.5
Disposable funds	14	17.5	14.5	14.7	9.1	8.1	5.8	8.7	6.5	6.3	6.3	7.9	10.1	10.3	12.3
Other funds	4	6.3	6.7	7.2	7.2	6.9	6.5	7.1	7.6	7.2	7.7	7.7	7.0	7.3	6.8
Available funds	18	23.8	21.2	21.8	16.4	15.0	12.3	15.8	14.1	13.5	14.0	15.6	17.1	17.6	19.2
For investment	10	11.4	11.0	10.2	10.2	9.7	10.3	11.0	11.6	12.2	12.5	12.0	13.0	12.7	12.6
R&D and innovation	6	6.7	6.9	6.7	7.0	6.8	6.7	7.2	7.5	7.5	8.0	7.9	8.4	8.4	8.1
Fixed capital	4	4.7	4.1	3.5	3.2	2.8	3.6	3.8	4.1	4.7	4.5	4.1	4.6	4.3	4.6
Surplus/deficit	8	12.5	10.2	11.6	6.2	5.3	2.0	4.8	2.4	1.3	1.5	3.6	4.1	4.9	6.5
Value added	50	53.4	50.2	51.3	49.6	45.9	46.1	46.2	45.3	45.3	45.7	45.9	47.0	45.7	46.2
Debt															
Total		51.9	52.4	54.3	54.8	53.4	47.9	48.3	47.9	50.9	53.1	51.4	49.4	47.8	45.8
Short-term		36.1	37.9	40.9	41.9	42.0	37.1	37.6	37.9	40.1	42.0	40.4	37.9	36.5	35.4
Long-term		15.8	14.5	13.4	12.9	11.4	10.8	10.7	10.0	10.8	11.1	11.0	11.5	11.3	10.4

Source: Statistisches Bundesamt, *Kostenstruktur der Unternehmen im Investitionsgüter produzierenden Gewerbe* (Reihe 4.3.2),
Beschäftigte, Umsatz und Investitionen der Unternehmen und Betriebe (4.2.1), *Preise und Preisindizes für gewerbliche Produkte
(Erzeugerpreise)* - Facherie 17; Deutsche Bundesbank, *Monthly Report*, November and May; VDMA;
Stifterverband für die Deutsche Wissenschaft, *Forschung und Entwicklung in der Wirtschaft, 1972 to 1985*

Table C3   Pattern of costs in the mechanical engineering industry in the United States: as a percentage of the value of sales

	Norm	1972	1973	1974	1975	1976	1977	1978	1979	1980	1981	1982	1983	1984	1985
For current output	86	94.2	94.7	94.4	93.4	99.4	92.5	92.9	93.4	94.2	94.2	92.2	96.8	97.6	97.2
Materials	40	41.1	42.7	44.4	44.1	50.1	43.2	44.1	44.1	43.3	42.5	36.3	40.8	41.1	40.9
Employment costs	32	32.2	32.0	30.9	29.6	29.4	29.8	29.1	29.1	30.3	29.1	31.9	31.1	29.6	29.5
wages & salaries		27.9	27.5	26.5	25.0	24.6	24.5	24.2	24.1	25.1	23.9	25.1	25.1	24.0	24.0
social costs		4.3	4.5	4.4	4.6	4.8	5.2	4.9	5.0	5.3	5.2	6.8	6.0	5.6	5.5
Industrial services	4	2.1	2.2	2.3	2.4	2.4	2.5	2.8	2.9	2.9	3.0	3.0	3.4	3.0	3.0
Other services	6	11.6	10.3	9.6	9.9	9.7	8.8	8.6	9.1	9.6	10.7	12.7	13.3	15.6	15.5
Interest payments	2	1.6	1.7	2.1	2.0	1.8	1.9	1.9	2.2	2.8	3.3	4.0	3.9	3.9	3.9
Taxes	2	5.6	5.8	5.1	5.4	6.0	6.4	6.3	6.0	5.2	5.7	4.3	4.3	4.4	4.4
Disposable funds	14	5.8	5.3	5.6	6.6	0.6	7.5	7.1	6.6	5.8	5.8	7.8	3.2	2.4	2.8
Other funds	4	6.6	6.3	5.4	5.6	5.6	6.5	6.1	6.5	6.7	7.7	9.0	7.8	6.1	6.0
Available funds	18	12.4	11.7	10.9	12.2	6.2	14.0	13.2	13.1	12.5	13.5	16.7	11.0	8.5	8.7
For investment	10	7.5	7.3	8.0	7.9	7.7	8.0	8.3	8.2	9.0	9.2	9.9	7.8	8.4	8.6
R&D and innovation	6	3.9	3.9	3.8	3.9	4.1	4.1	4.2	3.8	4.4	4.7	5.3	4.9	4.9	4.9
Fixed capital	4	3.6	3.3	4.2	4.0	3.6	3.9	4.1	4.4	4.6	4.5	4.6	3.0	3.5	3.7
Surplus/deficit	8	4.9	4.4	3.0	4.3	-1.5	6.0	4.9	4.9	3.5	4.4	6.8	3.2	0.1	0.1
Value added	50	45.2	44.8	43.7	43.7	37.8	45.5	44.5	43.9	44.2	43.9	48.0	42.5	40.3	40.5

Source: US Department of Commerce: Bureau of the Census, *Census of Manufactures, Census of Manufactures 1972, 1977 and 1982* and *Annual Survey of Manufactures*; Bureau of Economic Analysis, *Survey of Current Business*; Department of the Treasury, Internal Revenue Service, *Statistics of Income*; National Science Foundation, *Research and Development in Industry*; National Science Board, *Science Indicators. The 1985 Report*

Table C4   Pattern of costs in the mechanical engineering industry in Japan: as a percentage of the value of sales

	Norm	1972	1973	1974	1975	1976	1977	1978	1979	1980	1981	1982	1983	1984	1985
For current output	86	95.5	94.4	94.1	95.6	96.9	95.4	93.7	94.4	95.6	93.1	91.9	92.5	94.4	95.0
Materials	40	43.2	47.0	47.7	43.6	44.6	46.4	46.1	46.9	49.2	46.9	45.4	45.8	45.5	45.2
Employment costs	32	20.1	19.1	19.0	20.5	22.1	20.2	20.1	18.9	18.1	17.5	17.8	18.4	18.8	18.5
wages & salaries		17.7	16.8	16.9	17.8	19.4	17.3	17.0	15.9	15.5	14.7	15.1	15.6	16.3	15.7
social costs		2.4	2.3	2.1	2.7	2.7	3.0	3.2	3.0	2.6	2.8	2.7	2.8	2.5	2.8
Industrial services	4	10.5	11.1	11.1	9.6	8.8	11.0	11.5	11.8	12.9	13.0	12.6	12.5	10.7	11.1
Other services	6	14.9	10.8	8.8	14.4	14.4	11.4	10.3	10.9	9.2	9.3	10.2	9.9	13.5	14.7
Interest payments	2	3.8	3.4	4.1	4.5	4.2	3.7	2.9	2.5	2.9	2.9	2.6	2.9	2.6	2.4
Taxes	2	2.9	3.0	3.4	3.0	2.8	2.7	2.8	3.4	3.4	3.5	3.3	3.1	3.2	3.1
Disposable funds	14	4.5	5.6	5.9	4.4	3.1	4.6	6.3	5.6	4.4	6.9	8.1	7.5	5.6	5.0
Other funds	4	3.7	3.2	3.2	3.3	3.6	3.2	3.1	3.0	2.7	2.9	2.8	3.3	2.9	2.9
Available funds	18	8.2	8.8	9.2	7.7	6.7	7.8	9.4	8.6	7.1	9.8	10.9	10.8	8.5	7.9
For investment	10	7.0	6.9	7.9	6.5	5.9	6.8	6.6	6.8	7.5	7.9	8.5	8.6	8.0	8.9
R&D and innovation	6	3.0	2.9	3.4	3.1	3.2	4.0	3.7	3.7	3.8	3.9	4.3	4.7	4.5	4.4
Fixed capital	4	4.0	4.0	4.5	3.3	2.7	2.8	2.9	3.1	3.8	4.0	4.2	4.0	3.8	4.4
Surplus/deficit	8	1.2	1.9	1.3	1.2	0.8	1.0	2.8	1.8	-0.4	1.9	2.4	2.1	0.5	-1.0
Value added	50	31.4	31.1	32.4	32.4	32.2	31.2	32.1	30.4	28.8	30.8	31.8	31.8	30.2	29.1

Source: MITI, *Census of Manufactures: Report by Industries*; Ministry of Labour, *Yearbook of Labour Statistics*;
Statistics Bureau: Prime Minister's Office, *Report on the Survey of Research and Development*;
Bank of Japan, *Economic Statistics* - annual and monthly, *Price Indexes Annual*

Table C5 Pattern of costs in the electronics industry in the United Kingdom: as a percentage of the value of sales

	Norm	1972	1973	1974	1975	1976	1977	1978	1979	1980	1981	1982	1983	1984	1985
For current output	74	68.2	84.3	81.0	84.5	81.4	82.2	85.5	77.3	75.9	73.0	71.1	74.0	76.4	72.0
Materials	38	35.2	46.9	42.2	41.6	41.8	43.1	44.0	39.6	38.1	36.3	36.2	39.2	42.8	42.8
Employment costs	25	25.6	27.3	29.6	32.6	28.9	28.0	29.5	27.2	28.3	26.7	24.9	23.9	22.6	20.9
wages & salaries		23.3	24.8	26.8	29.1	25.7	24.7	25.6	23.4	24.3	23.0	21.6	20.8	19.8	18.4
social costs		2.3	2.5	2.8	3.4	3.3	3.4	4.0	3.9	4.0	3.7	3.4	3.1	2.9	2.5
Industrial services	3	1.2	2.5	2.3	2.5	2.3	2.5	3.7	3.8	3.4	3.5	3.2	3.5	3.3	3.0
Other services	2	1.7	0.9	1.6	1.9	2.2	2.1	3.0	1.9	1.5	1.4	1.3	2.1	2.0	0.3
Interest payments	2	1.5	1.4	1.6	1.3	1.1	1.3	1.2	1.7	2.0	1.7	1.5	1.2	1.3	1.3
Taxes	4	3.0	5.3	3.8	4.6	5.2	5.2	4.0	3.1	2.6	3.5	3.9	4.1	3.8	3.8
Disposable funds	26	31.8	15.7	19.0	15.5	18.6	17.8	14.6	22.7	24.1	27.0	29.0	26.0	23.7	28.0
Other funds	6	4.3	4.8	4.2	5.2	6.0	5.0	5.8	5.5	6.0	5.0	5.6	6.5	5.8	4.5
Available funds	32	36.1	20.4	23.2	20.7	24.6	22.9	20.4	28.2	30.0	32.0	34.5	32.4	29.4	32.5
For investment	20	14.8	14.9	16.2	14.8	15.1	18.3	22.3	22.9	23.3	24.8	24.1	23.6	23.0	25.6
R&D and innovation	15	11.4	11.0	11.7	10.9	11.5	14.2	17.1	18.0	18.7	20.1	19.5	18.7	17.4	20.8
Fixed capital	5	3.4	3.9	4.6	3.9	3.7	4.1	5.2	5.0	4.6	4.8	4.6	4.9	5.7	4.9
Surplus/deficit	12	21.3	5.5	7.0	5.9	9.5	4.5	-1.9	5.3	6.7	7.1	10.5	8.8	6.4	6.8
Value added	57	61.9	49.7	53.9	54.0	53.7	52.3	49.3	54.7	57.0	58.9	59.3	55.1	51.9	54.0

Source: Department of Trade and Industry, Business Statistics Office, *Report on the Census of Production* (PA1002); *Company Finance* (MA3), *Overseas Transactions* (MA4), *Industrial Research and Development* (MO14), *British Business* - indices of output and prices; Board of Inland Revenue, *Inland Revenue Statistics* and special analyses

Table C6   Pattern of costs in the electronics industry in West Germany: as a percentage of the value of sales

	Norm	1975	1976	1977	1978	1979	1980	1981	1982	1983	1984	1985
For current output												
Materials	74	91.5	86.3	85.0	84.5	86.4	87.9	87.3	85.8	83.3	85.5	83.1
Employment costs	38	35.4	34.8	34.7	34.4	36.1	38.6	34.7	32.7	31.7	36.5	38.3
wages & salaries	25	37.8	36.4	36.4	35.8	36.8	37.0	37.4	38.1	36.6	35.1	33.0
social costs		31.2	29.8	30.3	29.8	30.6	30.4	31.2	30.6	28.9	28.1	26.4
Industrial services	3	6.7	6.6	6.1	6.0	6.2	6.6	6.2	7.4	7.8	7.0	6.6
Other services	2	1.9	1.7	1.8	1.9	2.2	2.4	2.5	2.5	2.5	2.6	2.8
Interest payments	2	11.3	8.9	7.6	7.8	7.0	5.5	8.3	8.7	8.4	7.0	4.7
Taxes	4	3.0	2.9	2.9	2.9	2.8	2.7	2.3	2.2	2.4	2.8	2.7
Disposable funds	26	8.5	13.7	15.0	15.5	13.6	12.1	12.7	14.2	16.7	14.5	16.9
Other funds	6	9.8	10.0	9.8	9.3	9.9	9.8	11.7	16.3	12.2	11.0	10.8
Available funds	32	18.3	23.7	24.8	24.8	23.4	21.9	24.4	30.6	29.0	25.5	27.7
For investment												
R&D and innovation	20	16.3	19.0	17.4	19.9	20.1	20.3	20.8	21.4	21.0	21.2	24.2
Fixed capital	15	13.1	14.6	13.0	15.4	15.3	15.6	16.0	16.8	16.1	15.9	17.6
	5	3.2	4.5	4.4	4.5	4.7	4.8	4.9	4.6	4.9	5.3	6.5
Surplus/deficit	12	2.0	4.6	7.4	4.8	3.4	1.6	3.5	9.2	8.0	4.3	3.5
Value added	57	51.4	54.6	55.9	55.9	54.8	53.5	54.5	56.1	57.4	53.9	54.2

Source: Statistisches Bundesamt, *Kostenstruktur der Unternehmen im Investitionsgüter produzierenden Gewerbe* (Reihe 4.3.2), *Beschäftigte, Umsatz und Investitionen der Unternehmen und Betriebe* (4.2.1), *Preise und Preisindizes für gewerbliche Produkte (Erzeugerpreise)* - Fachserie 17; Deutsche Bundesbank, *Monthly Report*, November and May; Stifterverband für die Deutsche Wissenschaft, *Forschung und Entwicklung in der Wirtschaft, 1972 to 1985*

Table C7   Pattern of costs in the electronics industry in the United States: as a percentage of the value of sales

	Norm	1972	1973	1974	1975	1976	1977	1978	1979	1980	1981	1982	1983	1984	1985
For current output	74	80.9	83.9	84.8	83.6	83.4	81.2	83.9	82.0	84.4	82.4	84.9	82.8	83.4	83.2
Materials	38	37.3	38.2	39.1	37.9	37.2	36.9	37.7	38.8	38.4	36.4	36.2	35.3	36.6	36.4
Employment costs	25	31.0	31.5	31.6	31.8	30.6	29.4	30.9	29.7	29.7	29.7	30.1	30.3	28.0	28.2
wages & salaries		27.0	27.2	27.1	27.0	25.6	24.5	25.6	24.6	24.6	24.5	24.3	24.8	22.8	23.1
social costs		4.0	4.2	4.5	4.8	5.0	4.9	5.3	5.1	5.2	5.2	5.8	5.6	5.1	5.1
Industrial services	3	1.7	1.8	1.9	2.0	2.0	2.0	2.1	2.2	2.2	2.3	2.3	2.4	2.4	2.4
Other services	2	4.4	5.0	4.8	5.0	5.8	4.9	5.2	3.4	5.0	4.3	7.0	7.0	8.9	8.6
Interest payments	2	1.8	2.1	2.8	2.3	2.0	2.0	2.1	2.6	3.9	4.8	4.6	3.5	3.2	3.2
Taxes	4	4.7	5.3	4.6	4.7	5.9	6.0	5.8	5.4	5.1	5.0	4.7	4.4	4.5	4.5
Disposable funds	26	19.1	16.1	15.2	16.4	16.6	18.8	16.1	18.0	15.6	17.6	15.1	17.2	16.6	16.8
Other funds	6	7.0	7.1	7.1	8.3	8.8	9.5	9.2	8.5	9.9	12.3	10.3	11.0	9.2	10.2
Available funds	32	26.1	23.2	22.4	24.7	25.4	28.3	25.3	26.5	25.5	29.9	25.4	28.3	25.8	27.0
For investment	20	18.8	18.2	17.9	17.0	16.7	15.7	16.5	17.8	19.1	20.0	20.6	20.6	22.8	23.6
R&D and innovation	15	16.1	14.3	13.5	13.9	13.2	12.1	12.0	12.6	12.9	14.2	14.4	15.0	15.8	16.7
Fixed capital	5	2.6	3.8	4.4	3.2	3.4	3.6	4.5	5.2	6.3	5.8	6.3	5.6	6.9	6.9
Surplus/deficit	12	7.4	5.0	4.4	7.6	8.8	12.6	8.7	8.7	6.4	9.9	6.2	7.7	3.0	3.4
Value added	57	56.6	55.0	54.2	55.2	55.1	56.1	54.9	55.6	54.4	57.0	54.5	55.4	52.1	52.6

Source: US Department of Commerce: Bureau of the Census, *Census of Manufactures 1972, 1977 and 1982* and *Annual Survey of Manufactures*;   Bureau of Economic Analysis, *Survey of Current Business*;   Department of the Treasury, Internal Revenue Service, *Statistics of Income*; National Science Foundation, *Research and Development in Industry*; National Science Board, *Science Indicators. The 1985 Report*

Table C8   Pattern of costs structure of the electronics industry in Japan: as a percentage of the value of sales

	Norm	1972	1973	1974	1975	1976	1977	1978	1979	1980	1981	1982	1983	1984	1985
For current output	74	89.4	89.5	92.4	92.8	91.5	91.8	92.2	91.6	90.6	89.4	88.7	84.5	88.1	87.4
Materials	38	49.8	51.9	52.0	48.6	51.7	51.2	49.1	49.0	50.0	51.8	49.6	49.5	51.8	50.6
Employment costs	25	13.4	14.0	15.7	17.6	15.3	16.0	16.1	15.2	13.1	12.7	12.6	11.7	11.0	11.3
wages & salaries		11.7	12.3	13.7	15.3	13.3	13.8	13.8	13.1	11.3	10.9	10.8	10.1	9.5	9.6
social costs		1.7	1.8	2.0	2.3	2.0	2.1	2.3	2.1	1.8	1.8	1.8	1.7	1.5	1.7
Industrial services	3	6.2	6.7	6.9	6.8	7.5	7.3	7.3	7.7	8.1	8.4	8.3	8.3	8.8	8.5
Other services	2	14.1	11.1	12.2	14.0	11.2	12.2	14.8	14.6	14.3	11.0	13.0	9.8	11.0	12.5
Interest payments	2	2.5	2.3	3.0	3.5	2.6	2.3	1.9	1.7	1.9	1.7	1.7	1.5	1.3	1.4
Taxes	4	3.5	3.5	2.7	2.3	3.1	2.9	3.1	3.5	3.3	3.9	3.5	3.7	4.2	3.2
Disposable funds	26	10.6	10.5	7.6	7.2	8.5	8.2	7.8	8.4	9.4	10.6	11.3	15.5	11.9	12.6
Other funds	6	2.8	2.9	3.0	3.4	2.9	2.8	2.8	2.5	2.5	2.7	2.8	2.8	2.6	3.0
Available funds	32	13.5	13.4	10.6	10.6	11.4	11.0	10.6	10.8	11.9	13.2	14.1	18.3	14.4	15.6
For investment	20	8.9	11.3	10.4	9.8	10.3	9.7	9.7	10.4	11.9	12.4	13.5	13.1	14.0	15.0
R&D and innovation	15	6.2	7.6	6.7	7.2	6.5	6.1	6.5	6.7	7.3	7.1	8.0	8.1	7.4	8.3
Fixed capital	5	2.7	3.7	3.7	2.6	3.8	3.6	3.2	3.7	4.7	5.3	5.5	5.0	6.6	6.6
Surplus/deficit	12	4.5	2.2	0.2	0.8	1.1	1.3	0.9	0.5	0.0	0.9	0.7	5.2	0.5	0.6
Value added	57	30.0	30.4	29.0	30.7	29.5	29.3	28.8	28.7	27.6	28.9	29.1	32.4	28.4	28.4

Source: MITI, *Census of Manufactures: Report by Industries*; Ministry of Labour, *Yearbook of Labour Statistics*;
Statistics Bureau: Prime Minister's Office, *Report on the Survey of Research and Development*;
Bank of Japan, *Economic Statistics* - annual and monthly, *Price Indexes Annual*

Table C9   Pattern of costs in the motor vehicle industry in the United Kingdom: as a percentage of the value of sales

	Norm	1968	1972	1973	1974	1975	1976	1977	1978	1979	1980	1981	1982	1983	1984	1985
For current output	84	91.2	92.1	97.7	93.3	99.3	100.8	98.6	95.9	97.7	100.2	99.7	97.8	90.7	94.1	92.2
Materials	50	61.5	61.2	62.3	56.0	63.5	62.2	58.7	56.2	58.5	56.3	56.1	57.0	55.3	58.1	57.7
Employment	22	22.6	25.0	26.1	28.6	27.6	29.2	29.4	29.6	30.2	33.2	32.5	29.2	25.5	25.4	23.8
wages & salaries	20.8	23.1	25.8	26.1	24.7	25.6	25.4	25.2	25.6	28.2	27.5	24.9	21.8	22.2	20.9	
social costs	1.8	1.9	2.2	2.6	2.8	3.6	4.0	4.2	4.6	5.0	5.0	4.3	3.6	3.2	2.9	
Industrial services	2	1.6	1.7	1.7	1.7	1.5	1.7	1.9	1.9	1.0	1.1	1.0	1.7	1.6	1.7	1.9
Other services	6	2.0	2.0	1.9	2.5	2.6	2.9	3.3	3.7	4.6	5.7	6.2	6.1	5.3	5.9	6.1
Interest payments	2	1.7	1.3	1.6	2.4	2.5	2.2	1.6	1.6	2.0	2.8	2.6	2.2	2.0	1.9	1.7
Indirect taxes	1	0.6	0.5	0.5	0.8	0.8	0.8	0.8	0.7	0.7	0.9	1.1	1.1	1.0	1.0	0.9
Direct taxes	1	1.3	0.5	1.7	1.4	0.8	1.8	2.9	2.3	0.6	0.3	0.3	0.7	—	—	0.1
Disposable funds	16	8.8	8.0	2.3	6.7	0.7	-0.8	1.4	4.1	2.3	-0.2	0.3	2.2	9.3	5.9	7.8
Other funds	8	4.1	4.7	2.9	2.2	4.4	9.1	7.6	11.4	6.4	16.3	20.6	12.8	8.0	9.8	9.2
Available funds	24	12.9	12.8	5.2	8.9	5.2	8.4	8.9	15.5	8.7	16.1	20.9	15.0	17.3	15.8	17.0
For investment	12	7.3	6.8	7.7	8.2	7.1	7.3	8.2	9.0	11.5	11.4	10.2	11.4	12.0	13.1	12.6
R&D and innovation	8	4.0	4.3	3.9	3.7	3.7	3.7	3.9	3.6	3.9	4.4	4.8	6.0	6.0	7.4	7.7
Fixed capital	4	3.3	2.5	3.8	4.5	3.4	3.6	4.3	5.4	7.6	7.0	5.4	5.3	6.0	5.7	4.8
Surplus/deficit	12	5.6	6.9	-2.5	0.6	-1.9	1.1	0.7	6.4	-2.8	4.7	10.7	3.6	5.3	2.7	4.4
Value added	42	35.0	36.1	34.1	39.8	32.4	33.2	36.1	38.2	35.9	36.9	36.8	35.3	37.8	34.2	34.3

Source: Department of Trade and Industry, Business Statistics Office, *Report on the Census of Production* (PA1002); *Company Finance* (MA3), *Overseas Transactions* (MA4), *Industrial Research and Development* (MO14), *British Business* - indices of output and prices; Board of Inland Revenue, *Inland Revenue Statistics* and special analyses

Table C10 Pattern of costs in the motor vehicle industry in West Germany: as a percentage of the value of sales

	Norm	1974	1975	1976	1977	1978	1979	1980	1981	1982	1983	1984	1985
For current output	84	86.2	90.4	90.2	93.4	91.1	92.6	94.4	92.6	91.6	90.9	92.6	89.5
Materials	50	48.2	49.5	50.0	51.1	47.2	48.5	48.6	48.7	49.7	49.6	50.5	41.8
Employment costs	22	27.3	29.1	28.1	28.7	29.4	29.7	32.9	30.4	29.1	28.9	28.9	30.2
wages & salaries		22.6	24.3	22.8	23.5	24.2	24.6	26.4	25.1	23.8	23.3	23.4	24.9
social costs		4.7	4.8	5.4	5.1	5.1	5.0	6.5	5.3	5.2	5.5	5.5	5.3
Industrial services	2	2.4	2.6	2.9	2.9	3.1	3.3	3.4	3.3	3.4	3.5	3.6	4.0
Other services	6	5.1	5.3	4.7	4.8	5.5	5.2	5.5	5.7	5.3	4.9	5.5	8.1
Interest payments	2	1.2	1.2	0.8	0.8	0.7	0.7	1.0	1.4	1.2	0.8	0.8	0.7
Taxes	2	2.0	2.8	3.7	5.1	5.1	5.1	3.0	3.1	3.0	3.1	3.2	3.7
Disposable funds	16	13.8	9.6	9.8	6.6	8.9	7.4	5.6	7.4	8.4	9.1	7.4	10.5
Other funds	8	5.5	5.2	5.7	7.1	6.2	6.8	7.6	7.8	8.8	8.7	9.8	8.4
Available funds	24	19.3	14.8	15.5	13.7	15.1	14.2	13.1	15.2	17.2	17.8	17.2	18.9
For investment	12	11.6	10.0	8.8	9.9	10.9	12.0	14.1	13.6	14.3	14.0	13.1	14.6
R&D and innovation	8	6.0	5.8	5.3	5.4	6.0	6.0	7.1	6.9	7.1	7.3	7.5	8.6
Fixed capital	4	5.5	4.1	3.5	4.5	4.9	6.0	7.0	6.7	7.2	6.7	5.7	6.1
Surplus/deficit	12	7.7	4.8	6.7	3.8	4.2	2.2	-1.0	1.6	2.9	3.9	4.1	4.2
Value added	42	44.3	42.6	42.4	41.2	44.1	42.9	42.4	42.2	41.6	42.0	40.4	46.1

Source: Statistisches Bundesamt, *Kostenstruktur der Unternehmen im Investitionsgüter produzierenden Gewerbe* (Reihe 4.3.2),
Beschäftigte, Umsatz und Investitionen der Unternehmen und Betriebe (4.2.1), *Preise und Preisindizes für gewerbliche Produkte
(Erzeugerpreise)* - Facherie 17; Deutsche Bundesbank, *Monthly Report*, November and May;
Stifterverband für die Deutsche Wissenschaft, *Forschung und Entwicklung in der Wirtschaft, 1972 to 1985*

Table C11 Pattern of costs in the motor vehicle industry in the United States: as a percentage of the value of sales

	Norm	1972	1973	1974	1975	1976	1977	1978	1979	1980	1981	1982	1983	1984	1985
For current output	84	90.9	92.0	92.6	95.0	96.4	96.9	97.5	96.9	98.5	100.6	99.8	96.9	97.2	96.3
Materials	50	64.8	65.4	67.1	68.1	67.6	67.9	67.8	67.1	68.2	67.9	67.1	66.8	68.0	67.6
Employment costs	22	15.7	15.3	15.8	15.0	14.7	15.0	15.1	15.2	16.2	15.6	15.1	13.0	13.0	12.6
wages & salaries		12.7	12.3	12.3	11.4	11.3	11.7	11.7	11.5	11.9	11.7	10.8	9.8	9.9	9.7
social costs		3.0	3.0	3.4	3.6	3.4	3.4	3.4	3.6	4.3	3.9	4.3	3.2	3.1	2.9
Industrial services	2	0.5	0.5	0.5	0.5	0.5	0.5	0.6	0.6	0.6	0.7	0.7	0.7	0.7	0.7
Other services	6	3.0	3.7	3.3	4.3	5.1	4.3	4.7	5.1	4.6	5.4	6.1	6.5	5.7	5.5
Interest payments	2	1.5	1.7	2.5	3.0	2.4	2.3	2.6	3.8	5.5	6.9	7.2	5.7	5.2	5.2
Taxes	2	5.3	5.3	3.4	4.1	6.0	6.8	6.9	5.2	3.3	4.1	3.7	4.2	4.7	4.7
Disposable funds	16	9.1	8.0	7.4	5.0	3.6	3.1	2.5	3.1	1.5	-0.6	0.2	3.1	2.8	3.8
Other funds	8	4.2	4.0	4.4	3.9	5.3	6.2	6.4	7.9	7.5	9.2	9.9	6.0	7.8	8.5
Available funds	24	13.3	12.0	11.8	8.9	8.9	9.3	8.9	11.0	9.0	8.6	10.1	9.1	10.6	12.3
For investment	12	8.9	8.4	10.0	8.6	7.2	8.1	8.6	10.1	14.4	15.7	12.4	8.5	9.0	10.9
R&D and innovation	8	6.5	6.8	7.4	7.1	6.2	6.1	6.3	7.3	9.7	8.6	9.0	7.9	7.2	8.1
Fixed capital	4	2.5	1.6	2.6	1.5	1.0	1.9	2.3	2.8	4.7	7.1	3.4	0.6	1.9	2.9
Surplus/deficit	12	4.4	3.6	1.9	0.3	1.7	1.3	0.3	0.9	-5.4	-7.1	-2.3	0.6	1.6	1.4
Value added	42	31.6	30.3	29.1	27.1	26.7	27.2	27.0	27.2	26.5	25.9	26.1	26.0	25.6	26.2

Source: US Department of Commerce: Bureau of the Census, *Census of Manufactures 1972, 1977 and 1982* and *Annual Survey of Manufactures*; Bureau of Economic Analysis, *Survey of Current Business*; Department of the Treasury, Internal Revenue Service, *Statistics of Income*; National Science Foundation, *Research and Development in Industry*; National Science Board, *Science Indicators. The 1985 Report*

Table C12   Pattern of costs in the motor vehicle industry in Japan: as a percentage of the value of sales

	Norm	1972	1973	1974	1975	1976	1977	1978	1979	1980	1981	1982	1983	1984	1985
For current output	84	92.4	91.7	92.1	93.6	93.2	92.6	92.1	91.9	91.6	91.5	89.9	90.7	90.9	89.7
Materials	50	66.4	61.8	64.7	64.4	62.5	63.1	63.9	63.6	65.6	65.0	63.6	62.4	63.1	62.9
Employment costs	22	11.5	11.0	11.3	11.9	11.8	11.1	11.0	11.0	10.4	9.9	10.3	10.3	10.1	10.0
wages & salaries		10.0	9.5	10.0	10.3	10.2	9.6	9.3	9.2	8.8	8.5	8.8	8.7	8.6	8.4
social costs		1.5	1.5	1.3	1.6	1.6	1.6	1.8	1.8	1.5	1.4	1.6	1.7	1.5	1.6
Industrial services	2	5.5	5.6	5.2	4.7	4.7	4.7	4.7	4.5	4.9	4.7	5.5	5.0	5.4	5.2
Other services	6	3.3	7.9	5.8	6.5	8.0	8.4	7.7	7.7	6.0	7.4	5.9	8.5	8.4	6.8
Interest payments	2	2.4	2.3	2.7	3.0	2.4	1.7	1.4	1.2	1.4	1.2	1.3	1.3	1.2	1.1
Taxes	2	3.2	3.1	2.5	3.2	3.8	3.6	3.5	3.8	3.4	3.2	3.3	3.2	2.8	3.8
Disposable funds	16	7.6	8.3	7.9	6.4	6.8	7.4	7.9	8.1	8.4	8.5	10.1	9.3	9.1	10.3
Other funds	8	3.3	3.0	2.9	3.2	3.0	2.6	2.3	2.2	2.2	2.2	2.3	2.3	2.3	2.3
Available funds	24	10.9	11.3	10.8	9.6	9.8	10.0	10.2	10.2	10.6	10.7	12.4	11.6	11.4	12.6
For investment	12	7.4	9.1	9.2	7.0	6.4	8.1	8.0	7.5	8.9	9.9	10.8	9.6	9.3	10.0
R&D and innovation	8	4.2	4.7	4.4	4.5	4.1	4.4	4.8	4.7	5.0	5.7	6.2	6.2	6.3	6.4
Fixed capital	4	3.2	4.5	4.7	2.5	2.3	3.8	3.3	2.8	3.9	4.2	4.5	3.4	3.0	3.6
Surplus/deficit	12	3.5	2.2	1.6	2.6	3.4	1.9	2.2	2.7	1.8	0.7	1.6	2.0	2.1	2.6
Value added	42	24.8	24.7	24.3	24.4	24.7	23.8	23.7	24.1	23.5	22.9	25.0	24.1	23.1	25.2

Source: MITI, *Census of Manufactures: Report by Industries;* Ministry of Labour, *Yearbook of Labour Statistics;*
Statistics Bureau: Prime Minister's Office, *Report on the Survey of Research and Development;*
Bank of Japan, *Economic Statistics* - annual and monthly, *Price Indexes Annual*

Table C13 Pattern of costs in the chemical industry in the United Kingdom, as a percentage of the value of sales

	Norm	1968	1972	1973	1974	1975	1976	1977	1978	1979	1980	1981	1982	1983	1984	1985
For current output	85	83.8	78.0	81.4	89.1	86.3	85.6	84.7	85.4	87.5	86.0	86.7	86.2	82.3	80.5	80.3
Materials	50	52.5	50.2	53.3	62.5	57.5	59.5	58.9	57.5	60.7	56.7	57.9	57.2	55.9	56.0	55.8
Employment costs	20	17.1	17.1	16.2	14.8	17.0	15.2	14.6	15.6	14.9	16.7	16.2	16.0	14.4	13.2	13.0
wages and salaries		15.2	15.1	14.3	12.9	14.6	12.9	12.2	13.0	12.3	13.5	13.3	13.1	11.9	11.0	10.9
social costs		1.9	2.0	1.9	1.9	2.4	2.3	2.4	2.6	2.6	3.1	2.9	2.9	2.5	2.2	2.1
Industrial services	2	1.9	2.0	2.5	2.4	2.4	2.3	2.4	2.5	2.6	2.4	2.1	2.4	2.3	2.2	2.1
Other services	8	5.2	3.7	4.6	4.4	4.6	4.6	4.9	5.4	5.3	5.5	5.9	6.1	5.6	5.8	5.5
Interest payments	2	2.0	2.1	2.5	2.5	2.4	2.1	2.1	2.0	2.2	2.8	2.8	2.6	2.1	1.5	2.0
Taxes	3	5.4	3.0	2.4	2.6	2.4	1.8	2.0	2.3	1.8	1.9	1.8	2.0	1.9	2.0	2.0
Disposable funds	15	16.2	22.0	18.6	10.9	13.7	14.4	15.3	14.6	12.5	14.0	13.3	13.8	17.7	19.5	19.7
Other funds	5	8.6	6.8	5.9	5.8	6.2	9.4	5.7	6.6	6.2	6.8	6.9	6.1	7.2	10.8	7.7
Available funds	20	24.8	28.8	24.5	16.7	19.9	23.8	21.0	21.2	18.7	20.8	20.2	19.9	25.0	30.3	27.4
For investment	14	11.9	11.4	9.9	9.3	12.4	11.5	11.5	13.5	12.7	13.3	12.1	12.1	12.1	11.6	13.2
R&D and innovation	9	5.1	5.6	5.3	4.7	5.5	5.1	5.5	5.8	6.0	6.6	6.8	7.0	7.3	7.1	7.5
Fixed capital	5	6.7	5.7	4.6	4.5	6.9	6.4	5.9	7.7	6.7	6.7	5.2	5.0	4.8	4.4	5.7
Surplus/deficit	6	12.9	17.4	14.6	7.4	7.5	12.3	9.4	7.7	6.0	7.5	8.1	7.8	12.9	18.7	14.2
Value added	40	40.7	44.1	39.7	30.7	35.4	33.5	33.9	34.5	31.4	35.4	34.1	34.4	36.2	36.1	36.6

Source: Department of Trade and Industry, Business Statistics Office, *Report on the Census of Production* (PA1002); *Company Finance* (MA3), *Overseas Transactions* (MA4), *Industrial Research and Development* (MO14), *British Business* - indices of output and prices; Board of Inland Revenue, *Inland Revenue Statistics* and special analyses

Table C14 Pattern of costs in the chemical industry in West Germany: as a percentage of the value of sales

	Norm	1975	1976	1977	1978	1979	1980	1981	1982	1983	1984	1985
For current output	85	83.2	88.0	88.3	87.2	89.6	90.8	90.8	88.9	87.7	88.5	88.6
Materials	50	40.4	46.1	45.2	44.1	47.8	47.8	49.0	47.3	46.8	48.1	48.2
Employment costs	20	23.8	21.9	22.6	23.2	21.8	23.0	22.3	22.4	22.2	21.2	21.2
wages and salaries		19.7	17.8	18.4	19.0	17.5	18.5	18.1	18.1	17.3	16.5	16.7
social costs		4.1	4.1	4.1	4.2	4.3	4.4	4.2	4.3	4.9	4.7	4.8
Industrial services	2	3.4	3.6	3.9	3.8	3.9	4.0	3.7	3.5	3.2	3.3	3.5
Other services	8	10.8	11.4	11.7	11.2	11.0	11.2	11.4	11.4	11.5	11.7	11.2
Interest payments	2	2.0	1.6	1.6	1.4	1.3	1.5	1.8	1.6	1.1	0.9	1.0
Taxes	3	2.9	3.5	3.5	3.5	3.6	3.1	2.4	2.4	2.8	3.3	3.6
Disposable funds	15	16.8	12.0	11.7	12.8	10.4	9.2	9.2	11.1	12.3	11.5	11.4
Other funds	5	7.6	7.2	7.6	7.4	6.7	8.2	8.3	8.3	7.9	7.0	8.3
Available funds	20	24.4	19.3	19.2	20.2	17.1	17.3	17.6	19.5	20.2	18.4	19.7
For investment	14	14.0	13.1	13.4	13.5	12.5	13.3	13.4	13.3	12.9	12.3	13.2
R&D and innovation	9	7.8	7.8	7.8	8.4	7.6	8.0	8.4	8.6	8.3	8.0	8.6
Fixed capital	5	6.2	5.3	5.6	5.1	5.0	5.4	5.1	4.8	4.5	4.2	4.6
Surplus/deficit	6	10.4	6.2	5.8	6.6	4.7	4.0	4.2	6.2	7.3	6.1	6.5
Value added	40	45.3	39.0	39.3	40.9	37.3	36.9	35.9	37.7	38.5	36.9	37.1

Source: Statistisches Bundesamt, *Kostenstruktur der Unternehmen im Bergbau, Grundstoff- und Produktionsgütergewerbe* (Reihe 4.3.1),
Beschäftigte Umsatz und Investitionen der Unternehmen und Betriebe (4.2.1), *Preise und Preisindizes für gewerbliche Produkte -
Facherie 17*; Deutsche Bundesbank, *Monthly Report*, November and May; Stifterverband für die Deutsche Wissenschaft,
Forschung und Entwicklung in der Wirtschaft, 1972 to 1985

Appendix C

Table C15 Pattern of costs in the chemical industry in the United States: as a percentage of the value of sales

	Norm	1972	1973	1974	1975	1976	1977	1978	1979	1980	1981	1982	1983	1984	1985
For current output	85	81.1	79.9	82.9	83.9	83.5	87.1	87.7	85.9	88.2	89.4	91.8	89.5	90.2	87.1
Materials	50	41.0	41.4	46.9	47.6	47.7	50.3	50.4	50.6	52.5	54.2	51.8	50.5	50.5	47.5
Employment costs	20	15.4	14.9	12.9	12.8	12.2	12.3	12.5	11.9	11.8	11.3	12.5	12.0	11.4	11.4
wages & salaries		13.3	12.7	11.0	10.8	10.2	10.1	10.2	9.7	9.6	9.1	10.2	9.7	9.2	9.3
social costs		2.1	2.1	1.9	2.0	2.0	2.1	2.2	2.2	2.2	2.2	2.3	2.4	2.2	2.1
Industrial services	2	1.7	1.7	1.8	1.9	1.9	2.0	1.9	1.9	1.9	1.9	1.8	1.8	1.8	1.7
Other services	8	15.2	13.7	13.1	13.8	13.2	14.3	14.5	13.8	14.3	14.6	17.7	17.5	18.2	18.3
Interest payments	2	1.4	1.5	1.5	1.8	1.7	1.8	1.9	2.1	2.4	3.0	3.2	2.9	3.0	3.0
Taxes	3	6.4	6.8	6.7	6.1	6.7	6.5	6.4	5.6	5.2	4.5	4.8	4.9	5.3	5.3
Disposable funds	15	18.9	20.1	17.1	16.1	16.5	12.9	12.3	14.1	11.8	10.6	8.2	10.5	9.8	12.9
Other funds	5	6.6	7.1	7.2	7.4	7.7	8.3	8.3	8.3	8.6	9.4	9.3	9.4	8.4	8.2
Available funds	20	25.5	27.2	24.2	23.4	24.2	21.2	20.6	22.4	20.4	20.0	17.5	20.0	18.1	21.0
For investment	14	10.7	10.7	11.5	12.9	12.7	12.5	11.7	10.9	11.2	11.5	12.4	10.7	10.7	10.8
R&D and innovation	9	6.4	6.1	5.6	5.9	5.8	5.6	5.6	5.5	5.7	6.2	7.2	7.3	6.9	7.3
Fixed capital	5	4.3	4.5	5.9	7.1	6.8	7.0	6.2	5.4	5.5	5.3	5.2	3.4	3.8	3.5
Surplus/deficit	6	14.8	16.5	12.7	10.5	11.6	8.7	8.8	11.5	9.2	8.5	5.2	9.3	7.4	10.3
Value added	40	42.1	43.2	38.2	36.8	37.1	33.5	33.1	33.7	31.3	29.4	28.8	30.3	29.5	32.6

Source: US Department of Commerce: Bureau of the Census, *Census of Manufactures 1972, 1977 and 1982* and *Annual Survey of Manufactures*; Bureau of Economic Analysis, *Survey of Current Business*; Department of the Treasury, Internal Revenue Service, *Statistics of Income*; National Science Foundation, *Research and Development in Industry*; National Science Board, *Science Indicators. The 1985 Report*

Table C16 Pattern of costs in the chemical industry in Japan: as a percentage of the value of sales

	Norm	1972	1973	1974	1975	1976	1977	1978	1979	1980	1981	1982	1983	1984	1985
For current output	85	89.4	88.4	90.2	92.5	92.2	92.3	90.7	90.2	90.8	91.6	90.7	89.1	88.7	88.8
Materials	50	48.5	49.0	58.6	58.6	59.6	59.0	55.0	57.3	63.6	61.5	59.8	57.1	56.5	55.8
Employment costs	20	9.3	9.2	9.1	9.7	9.1	9.3	9.5	8.4	7.2	7.5	7.5	7.3	6.9	7.3
wages & salaries		8.0	7.9	7.7	8.3	7.8	7.7	7.8	6.9	6.0	6.2	6.2	6.1	5.8	5.9
social costs		1.3	1.3	1.4	1.4	1.4	1.5	1.6	1.4	1.2	1.3	1.3	1.2	1.1	1.3
Industrial services	2	1.9	2.0	2.3	2.3	2.2	2.2	2.3	2.2	2.2	2.2	2.3	2.4	2.4	2.4
Other services	8	22.3	20.5	12.7	15.3	14.7	15.5	17.6	16.0	11.6	13.8	15.1	16.2	16.8	17.2
Interest payments	2	4.6	3.9	4.1	4.6	4.2	3.7	3.3	2.8	3.3	3.6	3.0	2.9	2.6	2.5
Taxes	3	2.8	3.8	3.4	2.0	2.4	2.6	3.1	3.4	3.0	3.0	3.1	3.3	3.5	3.6
Disposable funds	15	10.6	11.6	9.8	7.5	7.8	7.7	9.3	9.8	9.2	8.4	9.3	10.9	11.3	11.2
Other funds	5	3.7	3.1	3.0	2.8	2.7	3.0	2.8	2.3	2.3	2.4	2.6	2.7	2.6	2.2
Available funds	20	14.3	14.7	12.8	10.3	10.5	10.7	12.1	12.1	11.5	10.9	12.0	13.5	13.9	13.4
For investment	14	14.7	10.8	11.2	13.8	11.0	10.0	9.8	9.0	9.2	10.1	11.0	11.3	11.0	11.8
R&D and innovation	9	6.2	5.6	5.3	5.4	5.2	5.4	5.5	5.8	5.5	6.0	6.6	7.1	7.4	7.9
Fixed capital	5	8.6	5.2	5.9	8.5	5.8	4.6	4.3	3.2	3.7	4.1	4.4	4.2	3.6	3.9
Surplus/deficit	6	-0.4	3.8	1.5	-3.5	-0.5	0.7	2.3	3.1	2.3	0.8	0.9	2.3	2.9	1.6
Value added	40	27.2	28.5	26.4	23.8	23.5	23.3	25.2	24.4	22.6	22.5	22.9	24.4	24.4	24.6

Source: MITI, *Census of Manufactures: Report by Industries*; Ministry of Labour, *Yearbook of Labour Statistics*; Statistics Bureau: Prime Minister's Office, *Report on the Survey of Research and Development*; Bank of Japan, *Economic Statistics* - annual and monthly, *Price Indexes Annual*

Table C17 Pattern of costs in the textile industry in the United Kingdom: as a percentage of the value of sales

	Norm	1972	1973	1974	1975	1976	1977	1978	1979	1980	1981	1982	1983	1984	1985
For current output	94	93.7	92.9	94.0	93.1	92.0	93.9	93.7	94.8	92.7	93.7	94.9	92.3	94.2	91.6
Materials	50	56.4	57.1	58.1	53.9	55.7	57.5	55.9	55.5	52.2	52.9	53.4	54.0	55.9	55.2
Employment costs	25	25.1	24.3	24.8	27.5	25.4	25.2	26.2	26.7	28.3	28.3	27.6	26.3	25.6	24.6
wages & salaries		23.1	22.3	22.6	24.8	22.8	22.3	22.8	23.2	24.5	24.3	23.9	23.0	22.6	21.9
social costs		2.0	2.0	2.2	2.7	2.6	2.9	3.4	3.5	3.9	3.9	3.7	3.3	3.0	2.7
Industrial services	4	4.9	4.4	4.3	4.5	4.3	4.5	4.5	4.7	3.9	3.7	3.6	3.6	3.3	3.6
Other services	9	3.7	3.6	3.1	3.6	3.3	3.6	3.7	3.9	4.3	4.7	4.7	4.7	4.6	4.5
Interest payments	2	1.7	1.8	2.2	2.1	1.9	1.7	1.6	1.9	2.4	2.5	3.7	2.2	3.2	1.6
Taxes	4	1.8	1.7	1.6	1.6	1.4	1.4	1.8	2.1	1.7	1.6	1.9	1.5	1.6	1.9
Disposable funds	6	6.4	7.1	6.0	6.9	8.0	6.1	6.3	5.2	7.3	6.3	5.1	7.7	5.8	8.4
Other funds	4	2.6	2.8	3.2	2.3	3.2	2.5	0.9	2.4	2.5	2.9	6.5	6.2	6.7	4.4
Available funds	10	8.9	9.9	9.2	9.2	11.2	8.6	7.2	7.6	9.8	9.2	11.6	13.9	12.5	12.8
For investment	6	4.7	5.9	6.0	4.9	4.1	4.0	4.8	4.9	4.6	4.1	4.4	4.5	5.1	5.3
R&D and innovation	2	0.5	0.5	0.6	0.7	0.6	0.5	0.5	0.6	0.7	0.7	0.8	0.9	0.9	0.8
Fixed capital	4	4.1	5.3	5.4	4.3	3.5	3.5	4.3	4.3	3.9	3.4	3.7	3.7	4.2	4.5
Surplus/deficit	4	4.3	4.0	3.2	4.3	7.1	4.6	2.4	2.7	5.2	5.1	7.2	9.4	7.4	7.5
Value added	37	35.0	34.9	34.5	38.0	36.7	34.4	35.9	35.8	39.7	38.7	38.2	37.7	36.1	36.6

Source: Department of Trade and Industry, Business Statistics Office, *Report on the Census of Production* (PA1002); *Company Finance* (MA3), *Overseas Transactions* (MA4), *Industrial Research and Development* (MO14), *British Business* - indices of output and prices; Board of Inland Revenue, *Inland Revenue Statistics* and special analyses

Table C18 Pattern of costs in the textile industry in West Germany: as a percentage of the value of sales

	Norm	1975	1976	1977	1978	1979	1980	1981	1982	1983	1984	1985
For current output	94	93.9	95.9	95.4	94.6	95.8	97.8	98.4	97.2	97.0	97.0	95.5
Materials	50	45.5	49.3	48.3	46.5	48.4	48.5	48.2	48.0	49.4	50.8	50.3
Employment costs	25	30.7	29.5	30.0	30.2	29.9	30.4	30.5	29.6	28.7	27.9	26.6
wages and salaries		25.9	24.7	25.2	25.4	25.1	25.5	25.5	24.7	23.8	23.0	21.9
social costs		4.8	4.8	4.8	4.8	4.9	4.9	5.1	5.0	5.0	5.0	4.7
Industrial services	4	6.3	6.5	6.7	7.1	7.1	7.5	7.2	7.2	7.1	7.1	7.4
Other services	9	7.3	6.9	6.9	7.1	6.7	7.2	7.9	7.9	7.9	7.6	7.6
Interest payments	2	2.2	1.8	1.7	1.7	1.6	2.4	3.0	2.9	2.0	1.8	1.8
Taxes	4	1.8	1.9	1.8	2.0	2.0	1.7	1.6	1.5	1.8	1.7	1.6
Disposable funds	6	6.1	4.1	4.6	5.4	4.2	2.2	1.6	2.8	3.0	3.0	4.5
Other funds	4	6.4	6.3	5.9	5.9	6.1	6.9	6.9	6.6	6.7	5.9	6.1
Available funds	10	12.5	10.4	10.5	11.4	10.3	9.1	8.6	9.3	9.7	9.0	10.7
For investment	6	4.9	5.3	5.3	5.2	6.0	5.8	5.1	5.3	6.3	6.0	6.4
R&D and innovation	2	0.7	0.7	0.7	0.9	1.0	1.0	1.0	1.0	1.1	1.1	1.1
Fixed capital	4	4.2	4.5	4.5	4.4	5.0	4.9	4.1	4.3	5.2	4.9	5.3
Surplus/deficit	4	7.6	5.1	5.2	6.1	4.3	3.3	3.5	4.0	3.4	3.0	4.3
Value added	37	40.9	37.2	38.1	39.4	37.8	36.8	36.7	36.9	35.6	34.5	34.7

Source: Statistisches Bundesamt, *Kostenstruktur der Unternehmen im Verbrauchsgüter produzierenden Gewerbe und im Nahrungs- und Genussmittelgewerbe* (Reihe 4.3.3), *Beschäftigte, Umsatz und Investitionen der Unternehmen und Betriebe* (4.2.1), *Preise und Preisindizes für gewerbliche Produkte (Erzeugerpreise)* - Fachserie 17; Deutsche Bundesbank, *Monthly Report*, November and May; Stifterverband für die Deutsche Wissenschaft, *Forschung und Entwicklung in der Wirtschaft, 1972 to 1985*

Table C19 Pattern of costs in the textile industry in the United States: as a percentage of the value of sales

	Norm	1972	1973	1974	1975	1976	1977	1978	1979	1980	1981	1982	1983	1984	1985
For current output	94	98.8	96.8	99.2	98.7	98.8	97.9	94.6	96.6	97.4	93.5	98.4	97.2	97.5	98.1
Materials	50	55.0	54.4	57.7	57.3	58.0	58.5	55.2	57.5	57.9	54.5	57.8	58.2	58.1	58.0
Emloyment costs	25	25.2	23.9	22.9	23.2	23.0	22.5	22.9	22.7	22.6	22.3	22.2	22.1	21.5	22.1
wages & salaries		23.0	21.3	20.4	20.6	20.3	19.5	19.8	19.5	19.5	19.0	18.9	18.7	18.1	18.7
social costs		2.3	2.5	2.5	2.6	2.7	3.0	3.1	3.2	3.1	3.2	3.3	3.4	3.4	3.5
Industrial services	4	4.8	4.5	4.5	4.3	4.1	3.9	3.7	3.5	3.4	3.1	3.0	3.1	3.1	3.1
Other services	9	8.2	7.9	8.2	8.5	8.0	7.3	6.7	6.9	7.6	7.6	9.3	8.6	8.5	8.6
Interest payments	2	1.4	1.6	2.0	1.7	1.4	1.3	1.4	1.7	1.8	2.1	2.2	1.9	2.3	2.3
Taxes	4	4.2	4.4	4.0	3.7	4.3	4.4	4.7	4.4	4.1	3.9	3.9	3.3	4.0	4.0
Disposable funds	6	1.2	3.2	0.8	1.3	1.2	2.1	5.4	3.4	2.6	6.5	1.6	2.8	2.5	1.9
Other funds	4	3.4	3.5	3.3	3.4	3.5	3.5	3.7	3.8	4.1	4.3	4.6	4.5	4.0	3.9
Available funds	10	4.6	6.7	4.1	4.8	4.7	5.6	9.1	7.2	6.7	10.8	6.2	7.3	6.5	5.8
For investment	6	5.3	4.8	4.8	4.4	4.2	4.2	4.4	4.1	4.4	4.6	4.6	4.2	5.2	4.7
R&D and innovation	2	0.7	0.6	0.7	0.7	0.7	0.6	0.7	0.7	0.7	0.7	0.8	0.8	1.1	0.8
Fixed capital	4	4.6	4.2	4.1	3.7	3.5	3.5	3.7	3.4	3.7	3.9	3.8	3.4	4.1	4.0
Surplus/deficit	4	-0.7	1.8	-0.7	0.3	0.6	1.5	4.7	3.1	2.3	6.2	1.6	3.1	1.2	1.1
Value added	37	32.0	33.1	29.6	29.9	29.9	30.3	34.4	32.1	31.2	34.9	29.9	30.1	30.3	30.3

Source: US Department of Commerce: Bureau of the Census, *Census of Manufactures 1972, 1977 and 1982 and Annual Survey of Manufactures*; Bureau of Economic Analysis, *Survey of Current Business*; Department of the Treasury, Internal Revenue Service, *Statistics of Income*; National Science Foundation, *Research and Development in Industry*; National Science Board, *Science Indicators. The 1985 Report*

Table 20   Pattern of costs in the textile industry in Japan: as a percentage of the value of sales

	Norm	1972	1973	1974	1975	1976	1977	1978	1979	1980	1981	1982	1983	1984	1985
For current output	94	95.6	93.2	98.8	99.2	97.5	98.6	97.6	94.9	96.6	96.2	96.3	96.7	95.3	97.3
Materials	50	55.0	54.9	56.6	55.7	56.3	56.4	54.1	53.7	55.2	55.1	55.2	54.5	54.1	54.2
Employment costs	25	17.5	16.3	18.7	19.2	18.1	19.1	19.3	18.6	18.1	18.4	18.7	19.1	19.0	19.9
wages & salaries		15.3	14.3	16.4	16.6	15.8	16.5	16.6	16.2	15.8	16.0	16.1	16.5	16.4	16.9
social costs		2.2	2.1	2.3	2.6	2.3	2.6	2.8	2.5	2.3	2.4	2.6	2.5	2.6	2.9
Industrial services	4	7.3	7.2	6.9	7.1	6.7	6.9	6.8	7.2	7.1	7.6	7.6	7.6	7.6	7.6
Other services	9	10.4	8.8	10.2	11.0	10.3	10.6	12.0	10.4	11.0	9.7	9.6	10.6	9.4	11.0
Interest payments	2	3.7	3.2	4.6	4.9	4.3	4.2	3.8	3.1	3.7	3.8	3.6	3.5	3.4	3.0
Taxes	4	1.7	2.7	1.7	1.3	1.7	1.4	1.5	1.8	1.5	1.5	1.6	1.5	1.6	1.7
Disposable funds	6	4.4	6.8	1.2	0.8	2.5	1.4	2.4	5.1	3.4	3.8	3.7	3.3	4.7	2.7
Other funds	4	3.4	3.0	3.5	3.2	2.8	3.2	2.9	2.5	2.4	2.6	2.6	2.6	2.5	2.1
Available funds	10	7.7	9.7	4.7	4.0	5.4	4.6	5.4	7.7	5.8	6.4	6.3	5.9	7.2	4.8
For investment	6	5.2	5.1	4.8	3.8	3.4	3.2	2.9	3.7	3.6	4.4	4.4	4.2	4.6	4.0
R&D and innovation	2	0.7	1.0	0.8	0.9	0.7	0.7	0.9	1.2	1.1	2.2	1.7	1.8	2.0	1.6
Fixed capital	4	4.4	4.1	4.0	2.8	2.6	2.5	2.0	2.5	2.5	2.2	2.8	2.4	2.6	2.3
Surplus/deficit	4	2.6	4.7	-0.2	0.2	2.0	1.4	2.5	4.0	2.2	2.0	1.9	1.7	2.6	0.8
Value added	37	27.3	29.1	26.3	26.3	26.7	26.1	27.1	28.7	26.6	27.6	27.6	27.3	28.8	27.3

Source: MITI, *Census of Manufactures: Report by Industries*; Ministry of Labour, *Yearbook of Labour Statistics*;
Statistics Bureau: Prime Minister's Office, *Report on the Survey of Research and Development*;
Bank of Japan, *Economic Statistics* - annual and monthly, *Price Indexes Annual*

Government policies

Government measures in the United Kingdom from 1945 to 1980

The post-war reconstruction plans in the United Kingdom were built around the principle of fairness for all classes with special attention being paid to those who had suffered during the hostilities. In addition reconstruction was broadened to include health, housing and education, all to a much higher standard and controlled directly by government. Plans were made and executed and the reputations of government ministers relied on the number of new houses built, hospitals commissioned or primary schools opened to a new and modern design.

During this period, little attention was paid to industry by policy makers, except in so far as ministers were determined that firms should not be allowed to profit from the shortages and problems of the reconstruction period. To this end, raw materials could be obtained only on licence and, before 1952, precise product specifications were laid down by government departments under the 'utility' schemes. It followed that there was little or no room for innovation nor for the flexibility required to adjust to the post-war shortages. Furthermore, while British manufacturers remained in a straitjacket, their competitors on mainland Europe were making a rapid recovery, and their new and innovative products proved highly competitive in British markets.

With demobilisation incomplete, the extensive war damage repairs and the growing activity of the public sector, a shortage of labour was inevitable. A cost of living sliding scale was in operation; but between 1946 and 1948 earnings rose by 14.2 per cent.

Concern about the problem of rising earnings was responsible for the first White Paper in February 1948, *Personnel, Incomes, Costs and Prices*, which concluded that: 'There is no justification for any general increase of individual money incomes'. In October 1948 the 'Stafford Cripps wage freeze' was introduced. In September 1949, sterling was devalued and the cost of living sliding scale was abandoned.

From 1950 to 1979, an attempt was made by successive governments to restrain wages and prices. This was done by means of policy statements, with or without new statutory bodies. From 1957, when a Conservative Government was in power, these included the following:

August 1957 The Council on Prices, Productivity and Incomes

Conservatives win election – October 1959
February 1962 White Paper, *Incomes Policy, the Next Step*, (Guideline 2-2.5 per cent)
July 1962   National Incomes Commission

April 1964   Statement of Intent (Guideline 3.5 per cent)

Labour wins election – October 1964
December 1964   Joint Statement of Intent on Productivity, Prices and Incomes
February 1965   White Paper, *Machinery of Prices and Incomes Policy*
March 1965   National Board for Prices and Incomes (TUC agrees to 3-3.5 per
                            cent norm for wages increase)
April 1965   White Paper, *Prices and Incomes Policy* (Cmnd 2639)
November 1965   White Paper, *Prices and Incomes Policy: an Early Warning System*
                            (Cmnd 2808)
July 1965   White Paper, *Prices and Incomes Standstill Period of Severe
                            Restraint* (Cmnd 3073) Six month freeze

Labour wins election – March 1966
August 1966   Prices and Incomes Act 1966 passed
March 1967   White Paper, *Prices and Incomes Policy after 10 June 1967* (Cmnd
                            3235)
April 1968   White Paper, *Productivity, Prices and Incomes Policy in 1968 and
                            1969* (Cmnd 3590) This set ceiling of 3.5 per cent with productivity
                            exceptions
July 1968   Prices and Incomes Act 1968 became law
October 1969   National Board for Prices and Incomes to be merged with
                            Monopolies Commission in a new Commission for Industry and
                            Manpower
December 1969   White Paper, *Productivity, Prices and Incomes Policy after 1969*
                            (Cmnd 4237) Range for settlements 2.5-4.5 per cent (Actual:
                            explosion of wage settlements – in engineering 18 per cent)

Conservatives win election – June 1970
November 1970   Office of Manpower Economics established
February 1972   State of Emergency declared. 2-3 day week introduced
August 1973   CBI, TUC and Government discuss anti-inflation policy
November 1972   Counter-inflation (Temporary Provisions) Act 1972
                            Temporary wages standstill
                            White Paper, *A Programme for Controlling Inflation, The First
                            Stage* (Cmnd 5152)
January 1973   Pay Board and Prices Commission set up for three years under
                            Counter-Inflation Act 1973
February 1973   Green Paper, *The Price and Pay Code – a Consultative Document*
March 1973   Pay Board established
April 1973   White Paper, *The Counter-inflation Programme – The Operation
                            of Stage Two* (Cmnd 5267)
November 1973   New code on pay came into force
November 1973   State of Emergency declared

December 1973   Three-day week announced

Labour wins election – March 1974
July 1974   Pay Board abolished with all associated statutory controls on pay
September 1974   Social contract (Average wage increase 24 per cent)
July 1975   White Paper, *The Attack on Inflation* (Cmnd 6151)
May 1976   Price rises to be kept to 5 per cent for 6 months from 16 February
June 1976   White Paper, *The Attack on Inflation. The Second Year* Cmnd 6507
1977   The Price Commission Act 1977
April 1978   National Engineers' pay agreement. Lowest paid to move onto new minimum rates
July 1978   White Paper. *Winning the Battle against Inflation.*
                 (1) Productivity must be self-financing
                 (2) Price control to continue
January 1979   Government wages policy relaxed. More cash for the lower paid

Conservatives win election – May 1979
May 1979   The Notification Order of Price Code revoked with effect from 24 May
April 1980   Competition Act 1980
                 Repealed:
                 The Counter-Inflation Act 1973
                 The Prices Act 1974
                 The Price Commission Act 1977 and (Amendment) Act 1979

Price control and its effects on innovation

Price control, its objectives and its effects, have been mentioned in the description of the performance of British industry. Further discussion is required because Britain is the only country of those studied where pricing policy was overseen by civil servants for the best part of 35 years. It is of interest that French industry is in the same situation and the findings (including those of the economists at the OECD) have shown very similar results to those in Britain.

Price control was finally removed by the Competition Act in 1980. As this was nine years ago, it is easy to assume that its effects have long since disappeared. But this is not so. Research and innovation are still funded out of the discretionary funds, that is the funds remaining after all disbursements for current production have been made – the 'disposable funds' as they appear in the tables. It follows that, if disposable funds are reduced, then intangible investment is directly affected, and the damage to product development is cumulative.

It should be noted that the implementation of counter-inflationary policies was over a very long period, from 1948 to 1979. Some of the worst aspects are described in *Price Controls and the Price Commission: The Business View*, CBI, May 1979. It concluded:

> There is no doubt that the price control rules of the Price Code were not the answer: on the contrary they created conditions which were seriously anti-competitive in their effect.

The general effects were insidious and cumulative; they added to industrial costs, an extra accountant was often needed to handle the paper work, they diverted attention away from the market and the activities of competitors and, most important of all, by denying companies the short-term premium price for innovative products, they reduced (sometimes obliterated) laboratories and design teams. This meant that price control depressed innovative activity just at a time when Japanese competition was building up.

In the early years, control had been intermittent, but from August 1966, following a six months freeze on prices, the *Prices and Incomes Act* was passed and was strengthened by the *Prices and Incomes Act 1968*. All British governments embraced these policies and in 1973 the control was further strengthened. The Pay Board and Prices Commission was set up under the Counter-Inflation Act 1973, with a staff of 250 in eighteen regional offices.

During all this period, output in mechanical engineering was rising, the peak coming in 1974. Nevertheless, between 1967 and 1973, R&D expenditure and manpower had been halved. The pattern of costs shows the details, disposable funds had fallen and the only offset had been a fall in taxation.

With this background, the first oil price shock was catastrophic. It raised the price of materials by 55 per cent, while price control held price increases down to 30 per cent. The comparison with Germany, where producer prices rose to meet the higher material costs, emphasises this point.

This evidence on its own and the consequent fall in R&D would have been serious enough, but it coincided with the rise in competitiveness of Japanese industry. With R&D held down over the previous 20 years and product development reduced accordingly – and unrewarded when successful – British industry had no reply. Between 1973 and 1982, output fell heavily and market share dropped from 11 per cent to 7 per cent.

With R&D manpower reduced from 20,000 in 1967 to 9,000, the mechanical engineering industry had inadequate financial or technological strength to answer the rising R&D employment in Japan and in Germany.

The result as seen in mechanical engineering, motor vehicles, electronics and textiles was a devastating fall in competitiveness. No combination of policies could have been devised that so effectively reduced the power to compete, especially at a time when industrial relations were exceedingly difficult.

With the passing of the Competition Act 1980, price control was removed but the accumulated deficits in research and innovation could not be corrected in the short term; plans for new products had to be brought forward and teams for research and product development rebuilt. The index of output suggests that two years were required for this turnaround; output fell for a further period before starting to rise. This is particularly clear in textiles – an industry heavily affected by competition from Asia – yet the price control plunge was reversed, and this despite the recession of 1980 and 1981. A very similar picture emerges for motor vehicles and electronics. Chemicals had suffered less loss of output than engineering, nevertheless growth was the lowest of the four countries. However, with the removal of price control, growth was resumed particularly in pharmaceuticals and speciality products and, by 1986, the industry was able to challenge that of Germany.

The influence of the City analysts, the requirement to maintain dividends (the so-called short-termism) has been discussed earlier; it proved a less than helpful influence for product development. The imposition of price control exaggerated the City effects particularly where labour was uncooperative.

Evaluation of R&D and innovation

It has been shown that disbursements for the future output of a company are an economic imperative – that is, in the absence of a flow of new scientific knowledge and the application of that knowledge, the industry falls behind its competitors and loses market share. Put another way, research provides the dynamic, the scientific information which is then studied and commercialised. It must be remembered also that any research project may give a negative answer, providing the information 'not this way' or 'not yet'. In Japan, MITI accepts that 40 per cent of the research funded by companies will not have an immediate application, but will be put on the shelf for use or guidance at a later date. Such research – the 40 per cent – is not considered a failure, for experience has shown that results are part of the stream of information essential to rapid product development.

For wider policy considerations the important thing to remember is that research results carried out by industry are normally the sole property of a particular company and, thus, are not available to other companies (unless released to customers as part of the sales package).

The study of the cash flow models has shown that, as the name implies, there is a flow of cash allocated to R&D and a further one for innovation or commercialisation which includes market studies, product design and manufacturing start-up. The cash flow models reveal first that these disbursements are substantial in high-tech industries and, second, that they are not one-off events, but flows within which various projects may be interacting. Evaluation of the combined functions of R&D and innovation is, in practice, an evaluation of the work of teams of people – scientists and technologists with their supporting technical staff and, equally essential, the company planners and experts in finance and market intelligence. So how should economists, or company boards, evaluate the work of these teams?

The first question to be asked is, what is the precise aim of their work? The simplest answer is the survival of the company. Translated this means, in terms of cash flow, two different things:

- on the revenue side: a product acceptable to the customers so that the price charged is high relative to costs (substantial 'disposable funds' result)
- on the cost side: the establishment of a process by which the goods are produced efficiently and the equipment is well maintained and updated.

To achieve the survival of the company, more is needed than the mere existence of a laboratory. Sir Alastair Pilkington in a paper to EIRMA, emphasised that[1]:

> In a company that believes in R&D the activity will be thoroughly integrated with the rest of the business. It will be an intrinsic part of the company's strategic thinking. It will, by its integration, infuse into the company the awareness of the importance of defining its future... Scientists will be helped to invent the right things for a company if they are integrated because this will help them to know and define what is worthwhile in the market place.

Thus evaluation becomes an evaluation of the whole company performance and this has been the subject of the study described in this book.

In evaluation, the revenue from sales is the first and most visible criterion; it comes at the frontier with the customer who provides the money; it encapsulates competitiveness. At this frontier there is much conceptual confusion. Many people see companies as welfare organisations, dedicated to raising the standard of living of the customers by selling cheaply, barely above costs. 'We may not be the best, but we are certainly the cheapest', was a claim made by some manufacturers in Britain in the 1970s, encouraged by people who despised profits. Simple arithmetic, using the figures from the cash flow models, shows why this has been a dangerous philosophy. Low prices breed low margins which, in turn, reduce the money available for employment, reduce recruitment of scientific manpower, and so inhibit scientific advance and product development. Customers become dissatisfied with an inferior product, demand falls, prices are discounted and the firm goes into liquidation.

Furthermore, it is a self-defeating exercise. Wealthy consumers in Japanese, German and American markets buy imported goods as cult items and high prices are no barrier; they are part of their attractiveness. Moreover, to sell in this elitist market the goods must be of the highest quality, incorporating the latest improvements and novelties and, to achieve this, R&D and innovation are the mainspring.

The second criterion of evaluation is cost, the sum of *all* the cost items for current output. Some costs are controllable by the entrepreneur (employment and services) and some are not (material purchases and taxes). In evaluation this distinction is very important. It is arguable that the margin added to material purchases (or gross earnings) is the most important element in evaluation for, in the absence of price control, the margin added as a percentage of sales is the measure most sensitive to scientific know-how and its application - it reflects the two critical skills of product design and canny purchasing[2].

Thus evaluation implies three techno-economic stages – excellence in product design brings the *potential* for high margins; the existence of good market intelligence captures the customers *to confirm* such high margins; and the high margins ensure that innovation continues.

There are, however, two macro-economic situations which can modify this. The first example concerns the discounted prices sometimes used by Japanese industry to gain market entrance, and the second is price control as used (before 1980) by successive governments in the United Kingdom. These circumstances raise a highly important point in evaluation. What is being evaluated? Is it the survival of the company or is it the underpinning of government policy?

Manufacturing industry occupies a unique forum, one where technology, economics and policy-making meet; and this fact presents problems. Added to such problems are those of time scale which haunt politicians. If legislation damages the commercial opportunities by raising costs or delaying the launch of the new products, this should be taken into account in evaluating R&D. In practice, this is extremely difficult; legislation will itself alter the base from which company decisions are made (projects cut, technologists dismissed or factories closed). The one possibility is to compare the pattern of costs over the period of evaluation with that of an earlier period. This, at the very least, would show first, the degree of cost distortion, and second, where the changes have been made. Only then could one assess whether the products were sold in the planned number and/or produced the expected increase in sales revenue, or gross earnings.

But there is another approach – the path taken by Japan – which is to attain technological advance at whatever cost in respect of material purchases, remuneration or the accumulation of debt. If the financial and social culture of the country means that some understand the economic logic and regard these features as acceptable, then R&D projects can be given a positive evaluation purely on the grounds of market share – even though, in Europe, they would fail on financial criteria.

The technological infrastructure

So far, we have discussed firms with a solid technological base – mainly those who spend on R&D including contract R&D. In Britain there are 950 of these out of 90,000 manufacturing companies, so the remainder must obtain their technology from elsewhere. These figures provide one argument for research laboratories owned or sponsored by government, including those in universities. It is an argument well understood in Japan where new MITI laboratories are being built to handle emerging technologies.

Staff of small and medium-sized firms are not expert in all modern techniques and processes; they never can be. Dutch and German authorities have experimented over the last 15 years to improve the means of technology transfer. But for government financial officers there remains the same problem – who makes the decisions? Whether civil servants, with their committees, are believed to be all-wise, or whether the research directors at the laboratories are seen as closer to the problems through their personal contacts with industry, the question of choice remains. What should be done and how should it be evaluated?

One thing is certain. Whatever the end results, these evaluations must proceed in two stages. First, in the light of all published data – with full historical comparisons and in the light of the current macro-economic policies. Second, the impressions gained should then be tested in the field.

There will never be a complete answer, but the imperative is to incorporate all available information in a structured programme of analysis so that comparisons can be made over time, and between countries.

References

1. European Industrial Research Management Association, Proceedings of the EIRMA annual conference, 1981, p.13.
2. In mechanical engineering firms in West Germany it has been observed that firms with less than 100 employees achieve a higher margin than larger firms – presumably a combination of close attention to customer needs and careful purchasing to avoid waste.

Appendix E

Sources of data on the flow of funds

Although the annual economic measurements are common to all, the agency collecting the annual material varies from country to country. For example, interest payments are reported to the Deutsche Bundesbank in West Germany, to the Ministry of Finance in Japan and to the Internal Revenue Service in the United States. The titles of the publications used in this analysis are listed below:

United Kingdom

Department of Trade and Industry, Business Statistics Office
Report on the census of production, 1963, 1968 and annual from 1970 (PA1002)
Company finance, Business Monitor, annual (MA3)
Overseas transactions, Business Monitor, annual (MA4)
Analysis of commodities imported and exported according to industry of which they are principal products, Business Monitor (MQ10)
Industrial research and development, expenditure and employment, Business Monitor (MQ14)
British Business (weekly)
Output of production industries, 26 August 1988
Output of engineering industries, 26 August 1988
Companies: insolvencies, 26 August 1988
Producer prices, annual averages, 6 May 1988
Royalty payments and earnings, 12 August 1988

Board of Inland Revenue
Inland Revenue Statistics (corporation tax) 1963 to 1979, and unpublished analyses from 1980

West Germany

Statistisches Bundesamt ,Wiesbaden
Kostenstruktur der Unternehmen im Bergbau Grundstoff-und Produktionsgutergewerbe (Reihe 4.3.1)
Kostenstruktur der Unternehmen im Investitionsgüter produzierenden Gewerbe (Reihe 4.3.2)
Kostenstruktur der Unternehmen im Verbrauchsgüter produzierenden Gewerbe und im Nahrungs- und Genussmittelgewerbe (Reihe 4.3.3)
Beschättigte, Umsatz und Investitioner der Unternehmen und Betriebe im Bergbau und im Verarbeitenden Gewerbe (Reihe 4.2.1)

Preise und Preisindizes für gewerbliche Produkte (Eizeugerpreise)
Index der Grundstoffpreise
Deutsche Bundesbank
Monthly report of the Deutsche Bundesbank (November and May)
Jahresabschlüsse der Unternehem in der Bundesrepublik Deutschland, 1965 to 1985
Stifterverband für die Deutsche Wissenschaft
Forschung und Entwicklung in der Wirtschaft, 1975 to 1985
Verband Deutscher Maschinen- und Anlagenbau (VDMA)
Statistisches Handbuch für den Machinenbau, 1978, 1982, 1986

The United States

US Department of Commerce: Bureau of the Census
Census of manufactures: industry series 1972, 1977 and 1982
Annual survey of manufactures – statistics for industry groups and industries (including supplemental labour costs, 1973 to 1985)
Bureau of Economic Analysis
Survey of Current Business – Overseas investment (August volume)
Department of the Treasury: Internal Revenue Service
Statistics of income – corporation income tax returns, 1972 to 1985
National Science Foundation, Division of Science Resources Studies
Research and development in industry
Funds and scientists and engineers
Detailed statistical tables, 1957 to 1985
National Science Board
Science indicators. The 1985 report

Japan

Ministry of International Trade and Industry, Research and Statistics Department
Census of manufacturers, 1972 to 1985: *report by industries*
Ministry of Labour, Statistics and Information Department
Year Book of Labour Statistics
Statistics Bureau Prime Minister's Office
Report on the survey of research and development, 1973 to 1986
The Bank of Japan, Research and Statistics Department
Economics Statistics – annual and monthly
Price indexes annual – wholesale price indexes and export and import price indexes
Ministry of Finance, Security Bureau
Monthly Financial Statistics
Japan Statistical Yearbook
Automobile Manufacturers Association, Tokyo
Vehicle Statistics of Japan

Glossary and notes

Bankruptcy

A declaration by a court of law that an individual or company is insolvent, that is, it cannot meet its debts on the due dates.

Current costs

Disbursements for materials and components, employment, services, rent, interest payments and taxes for current output (line operations plus sales and administration).

Customer/contractor principle

Under the customer/contractor principle, as set out in the Rothschild Report and subsequently implemented by the then Government in 1972, government departments are placed in the position of customers for the research they need: the customer says what he wants; the contractor does it (if he can); and the customer pays. Substantial proportions of the funds previously received by the AFRC (then the Agricultural Research Council, ARC), MRC and NERC from the Science Budget were allocated instead to the departments concerned with research undertaken by the Council. The customer/contractor principle was to apply only to applied R&D; it was recognised that basic research '...has no analogous customer/contractor basis'.

This policy removed the decision making on research programmes from the directors of laboratories, who were in close touch with industry, to the Requirements Boards. As such R&D programmes were obligatory, the assistance given directly to industry was restricted and became subject to full economic cost instead of marginal cost.

Direct taxes

Income tax and corporation tax.

Disbursements

Money paid out by the manufacturer for materials, components, plant and equipment, for labour and outside services and for rent interest and taxes.

Disposable funds

The difference between the receipts from sales and the total of current disbursements.

Indirect taxes

Rates, vehicle licences, customs duties.

Investment
Expenditure on technological change comprises tangible and intangible investment.

Investment, intangible
(i) *Research and development*

(ii) *Innovation* (commercialisation)
Design of new products
Systems design
Market intelligence
Planning
Industrial engineering
Manufacturing start-up
Computer systems

(iii) *Licensing* of new technologies

(iv) *Training* of employees in –
professional expertise
information systems
re-training

Investment, tangible
(i) *Capital expenditure*
New building work
Land and existing buildings
Plant, machinery and vehicles
(ii) *Leasing* of plant and machinery

Konzertierte Aktion (Concerted Action)
Mutually agreed and consistent action by government, trade unions, employers' associations and farmers to achieve price stability, a high level of employment, stable foreign trade and an appropriate rate of growth, in accordance with paragraph 3 of the Stabilitätsgesetz (Stability Act). In 1964 the Sachverständigenrat zur Begutachtung der gesamtwirtschaftlichen Entwicklung (Council of Experts on Economic Development) recommended the adoption of this practice by the Federal Republic of Germany, on the model of other countries (English Social Contract, French Action Concertée). The proposal was briefly taken up by Economics Minister K. Schmücker but dropped; it was later implemented by his successor K. Schiller. In June 1977, when the employers' associations sought to have the 1976 Co-determination Act, which increased workers' representation on company boards, set aside by the Constitutional Court, the DGB (German trade union confederation) claimed that the basis for joint consultation had disappeared and ceased to attend konzertierte Aktion meetings.

Liquidation
The termination, dissolution or winding up of a limited company.

Loans
(i) West Germany
Short-term loans comprise, inter alia, accounts payable, liabilities on bills, debit balances on current accounts at banks, and down payments received. Debts to affiliates, unless they are recognisably long-term, are also included. The accounts payable, which are shown separately, include the liabilities on bills.

Long-term loans are debts with an original maturity of not less than four years. They include loans raised, mortgages, land charges in annuity and other forms, etc.

(ii) United Kingdom
Short-term loans are loans other than bank overdrafts which are wholly repayable within 5 years.

Long-term loans are loans, other than bank overdrafts which are not wholly repayable within 5 years.

Mintech
Ministry of Technology; 1964 to 1970 (United Kingdom).

MITI
Ministry of International Trade and Industry (Japan).

OECD/DSTI
Organisation for Economic Co-operation and Development: Directorate for Science, Technology and Industry.

Other funds
Funds received by companies other than those from the sales of goods produced. Examples are profits from merchanted goods, receipts from sales of unwanted plant and machinery, income from investments, investment funds from abroad, government grants.

Price Commission 1973 to 1980
An independent body set up by the British Government in 1973 to administer price control. In addition to administering the Price Code, the Commission reported on matters referred to it by the Government for investigation – such as motor fuel prices. It had eighteen regional offices and a staff of about 250. The regional offices investigated complaints about price increases and checked up on observance of the code.

The Notification Order 1978 was revoked with effect from 24 May 1979 as part of the Government's intention to introduce a new framework of competition policy. Consequently firms were no longer obliged to give advance notice of intended price increases and the Commission could not initiate any investigations under Section 4 of the 1977 Act.

Research Requirements Boards
In 1972 Research Requirements Boards were set up to operate in accordance with the Rothschild principle and act as proxy customers for the applied research of the Department

of Trade and Industry. The Boards approved projects and provided funds for contractors from industry, research councils and research associations, as well as the Department's own R&D establishments. In 1985 a new structure was introduced by which a single, high level Technology Requirements Board, supported by 16 advisory committees, provides advice to Ministers and the Departments' sponsoring divisions on all aspects of science and technology policy including advice on priorities between sectors and technologies (*The Penguin Dictionary of Economics*).

Sale-proceeds
Equivalent to the value of sales. Term used in J.M. Keynes, *The General Theory of Employment, Interest and Money*.

Sales, value of
All sales of goods produced (including those from materials given out) in the period of the enquiry irrespective of when goods were manufactured. The value shown for sales is the amount (excluding VAT) charged to customers after any trade discounts.

Services
Services performed by agencies or by individuals not employed by the company

(i) *Payments for industrial services*
Amounts payable to other firms for work done on materials supplied by the establishment, plus payments for repairs and maintenance.

(ii) *Miscellaneous* or *other services*
Rents of industrial and commercial buildings; hire of plant, machinery and vehicles (excluding leasing); bank charges, postal services, transport, advertising, professional services, bonuses and commissions.

Social Contract
Agreement with Trades Union Congress (TUC) in September 1974 on voluntary wage restraint, agreeing restricted wage increases and 12 month intervals between settlements.

Stop–Go
The description given to economic policy in the UK, particularly during the 1960s. The Government used fiscal and monetary controls to reduce aggregate demand, and so to preserve the exchange rate, which tended to come under severe pressure during boom conditions in the home market. These controls, together with the underlying trade cycle movements, produced subsequent periods of stagnation and rising unemployment, which, in turn, encouraged the Government to stimulate the economy, and so a return to boom conditions (*The Penguin Dictionary of Economics*).

Technological infrastructure
The complex of central laboratories, science parks, university research laboratories, consultants and government schemes of assistance set up with the objective of encouraging the transfer of new technology to industry and to public bodies.

Zaitech

Investment in the financial markets by the non-financial companies in Japan in order to boost income. This is a major preoccupation of companies that have a cash surplus, but includes other companies who have decided to supplement their meagre earnings with income from stock-market speculation – using funds borrowed at Japan's easy interest rates (*Investors Chronicle*, 1 May 1987).